Town of Stauffer's 4th of July celebration 1913. (Brookings photo).

— A MAVERICK PUBLICATION —

Oregon Outback

Russell Baehr

— A Maverick Publication —

Copyright © 1988 Russell Baehr

Library of Congress Number: 86-62476

ISBN: 0-89288-113-5

edited by Verne Reaves

cover photo of Russell Baehr by Denny Brown

published by
MAVERICK PUBLICATIONS
Drawer 5007 • Bend, Oregon 97708

Table of Contents

Preface

This book is but a faint echo of the past. It is missing many facets of a little known country. Yet, we hope, it will instill within the reader a curiosity and a desire to become better acquainted with that vast expanse of sky and land beyond the high Cascades which has been dubbed, *Oregon's Outback*. And for those who already know and enjoy the country, we have tried to capture something of the spirit of those who settled here.

It is an enchanting country. A harsh, but starkly beautiful land. And it grows on a person. It is a haunting land.

Some claim that sometimes, as you feel the desert wind flow and eddy over the sage and through the junipers, if you'll but stop and listen carefully you may catch a faint sound from the past.... A voice, a whisper, perhaps a cry from an early inhabitant. And that if you look closely you can see the dust raised by their tired feet as it blows and covers the relics of their bleak existance. Though we have but a diminished perspective of that time, you can still feel the pioneer's presence everywhere.

They gathered little material wealth over the years, those hundred old-timers the author visited with in the course of gathering stories of the Oregon outback. But each had a wealth of experiences, a deep appreciation of the land and its beauty, and warm memories of a host of friends they had gathered along the way. They were eager to share this love with you.

Contributors to the Manuscript

Jack Arnold, Boise Aune, Skip Bloomquist, C.A. Boyd, Edna Boyd Brinson, Mrs. Paul Brookings, Marie Brosterhous, Bill Burton, Mr. and Mrs. Busset, Mr. and Mrs. Grover Caldwell, Mr. and Mrs. J.L. Carter, Dave Cody, Mr. and Mrs. Joe Conniger,

Jim Cook, John Crampton, Mr. and Mrs. Manning Dickerson, Mr. and Mrs. Hugh Dugan, Mr. Hahlen, Dean Harris, Mrs. Jess Harter, Minnie Helfrich, Mr. Henderson (of Bend), Mrs. Henderson (of Culver), Mrs. Ray Hethorne, P.B. Johnson, Mrs. Jolley, Claude Kelley,

Karl Kleinfeldt, Mr. and Mrs. Kohfield, Jack Kribs, Mrs. McCaffery, Walt McCallum, Claude McCaulley, Mr. and Mrs. J. McClay, Mr. and Mrs. Walt McCoin, Ivan McGillvrays, Ray Markham, Jack Massart,

Roy Moffit, Cecil Moore, Mrs. Mortimer, Mrs. Mosley, John Munior, Arvilla Murphy, George Murphy, Clint Olson, Mr. and Mrs. W.C. Osborne, Slick Raper, Mr. and Mrs. Jim Read, Mr. and Mrs. Paul Riedel, J.R. Roberts, Mr. Sachrey, Mrs. Sanford, Sather Family, Rex Schroeder,

Gus Schuman, Mrs. H.A. Scoggins, Orissa Sears, Claude Seeds, Carl Settlemeyer, F.C. Settlemeyer, Dan Shannon, Mr. and Mrs. Cal Sherman, John Silvertooth, Mr. and Mrs. Glen Slack, Mr. and Mrs. A.E. Smith,

Marjorie Smith, The Steve Steidls, Earl Talbot, Jess Tetherow, Mrs. J.W. Thom, Bill Van Allen, Claude Vandevert, Emil Van Lake, Mr. and Mrs. Irving Walters, Charlie Weaver, Lonnie Weaver, W.C. Wood, Mrs. Workman, Mrs. Zumwalt.

Illustrations: Patricia Baehr, Chris Chambers, and May Baehr.

CHAPTER 1

The Setting

Geographically speaking, Oregon could have been two states. The beautiful Cascade Range divides it into two sections: the dry-siders to the east and the webfoots to the west.

It is a state of extremes, having its annual rainfall surpassed by only one other state, Washington, and its aridity by Arizona and New Mexico.

The peaks of the Cascades are unique as they march from south to north in a separate elegance seen in no other range in America. Central Oregonians have the box seat for viewing them. Most natives know the individual profiles by name.

This mountain range is the western boundary of our tale. Spreading east for miles and miles at the foot of them lies the juniper and sageland arena that is the heart of our story. The robust town of Shaniko to the north, the hamlet Burns to the east, and Summer Lake to the south roughly mark the three remaining edges of the region we are concerned with here.

This vast, semi-desert expanse lay unsettled since its forming except for wandering nomad Indian tribes.

Alaska had its gold rush, and California its forty-niners. The Cimarron and the Oklahoma Territories were both settled and cultivated. To the west, Oregon's lush Willamette and Santiam valleys had been under the plow for half a century.

Now, in the 1880's, the settlers were trickling in, from Shaniko, from valleys green, west of the mountains. Up terrible Seven Mile Hill and frightening McKenzie Pass they came. From the south, a few parties bypassed Linkville and headed into the Summer Lake-Silver Lake areas, called by many "the low desert."

Who were the people? What were they like? Why did they come?

They were the tired, the bored, the sick, and the enterprising. Many came to make their fortunes in this new land. Others, tired and bored at a 10-hour shift punctuated by a time clock, put in 16 hours on their own piece of ground, and rose each day with a zest for more.

A few left a past and wanted a new start. Some were running away from memories. Others came for health. Speculators, slickers, girlies there were, too.

Few who had wealth and comfort pulled up roots for this late frontier unless they had visions of riches in this land of promise. Yet this high, dry, frosty, sunny land had an invigorating climate if it had nothing else. It also had timber, virgin and almost boundless, bunchgrass and chamise for grazing sheep and cattle. Wild horses, mule deer, and antelope roamed the desert. Rivers ran white and green and pure, and lakes nestled deep and blue and tranquil in the eastern Oregon sun of many days.

Such was the setting that Fremont had passed through, recording its savage beauty in a diary almost forgotten.

CHAPTER 2

The Land

The country is fabulous.

That statement stands without an exclamation mark.

The land is flanked on the west by 10,000-foot peaks of the Cascades thrown up when some volcano did his bragging. It is slashed by an incredible series of malipai canyons to the north, carrying snow water to the mighty Columbia. The smaller tight-hilled and timbered Ochocos and Maury Mountains ring it to the east. Horse Ridge is the wharf of a desert basin that laps its way southeast into old Mexico.

South and east of Bend in scattered stands of huge ponderosas lies as fine a hunting country as there is west of the Rockies. Here, countless buttes raise their bald or timbered heads, their names adding, if possible, more color than they do with their own native beauty.

The mountains' immensity is permeated with evergreen smells, each fetchingly different. The jack pine flats give solitude and secretive surroundings, even as they close in behind one.

Dry juniper hills suggest gold nuggets, thunder eggs, and things petrified in hidden dry washes. A lone monarch of a juniper on a desert hill might be just the place for a cache of obsidian tips, hidden by a long-dead Indian scout.

The lava flows and outcrops of great tilted slabs, spiraled clinkers, lava bombs, and mile-long tunnels are mysteries in a place of pumice and cinders set in a world apart.

Miniature, cool, green lakes jewel the basins along the feet of alpine fir at timberline. They are strung together with foot trails where one can dip a drink as pure as God ever made.

In the high desert, lying between Burns and Bend, dry fathoms of a mysterious river, now choked by sand, wanders its way through miles of sage to spill down a cut of deep gorge at Horse Ridge. Then its diminishing perimeter heads to Powell Butte, and disappears.

There are two icy rivers springing up from the cool depths of the earth in huge springs. Fall River, some 20 miles southwest of Bend, and the equally exquisite Metolius, west of Sisters at Camp Sherman.

Fall River runs so limpid and pure that its colored sandy bottom can be seen for most of its length. Placid greens and eerie blue pad its bed in weed-forms hiding trout, while hillbilly shy in their wildness. An abundance of silvered pine copses bless its banks from either side as it chatters its way to the Deschutes. Elk, deer, coyote, and mink label its sandbars.

Though the local rivers start humbly in pastoral surroundings, they finally snarl their way through immense lava and basalt canyons baking in semi-desert suns, to flow to the mighty Columbia.

The Crooked River heads in the arid lands and broken rims of the desert, flows and flattens in its middle portion of farms, then storms past sheer canyon walls hundreds of feet high. Two new dams backwater it, creating Lakes Simtustus and Billy Chinook.

A sad note was added as one of the deeps crept over Cove State Park. This venerable spot nestling at the bottom of a deep canyon was so named by Clark Rogers almost a century ago. Pelton Dam's backwaters covered some 300 fruit trees with their fruit-laden history. For years, Alkali Ike filled his wagons and trekked his way up the precipitous wagon trails to bring the bounty of apples, pears, plums, and apricots to settlers

South of Bend near the Deschutes River. Possibly the McCoin family. (McCoin photo)

on the sage rims.

The last weekend it was open before flooding, this writer and his family watched mule deer saunter around munching on fallen apples.

As one Culver pioneer lady put it: If this is progress, they can have it!''

Wickiup Reservoir on the upper Deschutes got its name from the many wickiup rings and poles left from the transient homes of the Warm Springs and Klamath Indians. Outsize trout are pulled from Wickiup, Crane Prairie, East and Paulina Lakes. Their fame brings in scores of anglers every year.

The falls of the Big Deschutes, Pringle, Benham, and Dillon all have ample picnic spots for the visitors to behold their beauty.

The Little Deschutes starts far to the south near the birthplace of the Umpqua. They flow from the same height of land, one north and the other south. The Deschutes Rivers, Big and Little, flow two-thirds of the length of the state, covering many geologic locales and life zones. The Deschutes River system is one of the few in the United States that drains northward.

About 1900, an early settler known as Dutch John built his cabin on the acreage now known as River Bend Estates. His homestead was the gathering place of early Bend residents for periodic fish fries and venison feeds. One day, Dutch came up missing and another man started running his cattle. Since there were no specified lawmen at that time, it all went uninvestigated and in a few months it died a natural death. The one remembrance, a footbridge across the river there, stood until 1907, then partly collapsed. The timbers were aging on either side until the 1920's.

While the rivers were fine fishing for years, some of the remote mountain lakes were devoid of fish until fingerlings were hauled in by toboggan by Jess Tetherow and others of Redmond. Now they are stocked by low-flying planes each spring as soon as the ice melt is through.

In spite of fish trucks and planes, the lure is still there for anglers who hike to the remote outposts for a chance lunker. The print of a cougar or black bear, or the flash of an elk's rear end, can still highlight a trip to the mountain territory.

Some of these lakes are still little used. Only recently, the fifth largest lake, Waldo, had an improved road put into it. The Three

Sisters Wilderness Area is protected by law, forbidding motorized vehicles. Here the snarl of Hondas or Jeeps will not intrude on the solitude. From Crater Lake to Mount Jefferson, the delighted hiker can dip and drink, breathing air filled with little but pine scent and campfire smoke.

Small wonder the desert homesteaders dropped everything once a year to spend several weeks here, with the huckleberries, the Indians, and the patient mountains.

The high mountain lakes are trout waters, some expansive, some small jewels. With the advent of water-skiing, the larger ones are roped off to separate certain areas for fishermen. These alpine waters hold four species of trout — brown, eastern brook, cutthroat, and rainbow. It takes a pack string or good legs and lungs to reach some. Others lie a mile or so off the highway.

A unique tale telling of how one of these high lakes got its name was related by Rex Schroeder, a longtime resident of Bend.

He was in a party heading for Nash Lake down over the divide some three miles. As the men neared the Mirror Lakes group, they were entertained by the sight of four adults bathing in the nude in one of that cluster of lakes. On the return trip, one of the men, a lumberjack, gouged the name ''Denude Lake'' in a sizeable flat rock on the eastern shore, commemorating that colorful sight. To this day the name remains for the curious to seek out.

The Riddle brothers of La Pine and Rex made the trip in the early 1950's on the then-primitive Century Drive.

Throughout this area (Skyline Trail), a careful observer will note the large slabs of rock are all marked with striations from glacial activity. The Irish and Taylor Lakes sector have the identical grooves in the formations there, running northwest by southeast.

Hot springs were of special interest to the settlers, though not of much use for practical

Mouth of mile long Lava Cave, just east of Lava Butte. Now on the Deschutes National Forest. Note car at top right.

purposes.

Kahneeta Hot Springs is some 20 miles north of the Warm Springs Indian Agency headquarters. Another at Pringle Flat is in the desert located miles away, northeast of Brothers. Yet another bubbles out of popular East Lake at the southeast shore. This is in the Newberry Crater area of recent volcanic upheaval.

Other hot springs in the Lakeview region are used to heat dwellings, since they have the magnitude to be piped in. There are several in the Burns country, some of which had bath, picnic, and resort facilities in past years.

If hot springs don't interest you, how about an abundance of caves, some with ice, some without?

Arnold Ice Cave was so named when a traveler, Mr. Arnold, was on horseback heading for Bend. It was hot, and both rider and horse were suffering from lack of water. As they neared this spot, the horse took its head and stubbornly kept on course, and led Mr. Arnold to a large circular opening in the sage floor. Upon investigation, great globes of ice were seen receding in the cool dimness. Pattering of water in small pools greeted the man and his horse. This spot was to be one of the main sources of ice for Bend for several years. Countless wagonloads were brought in.

Another, Edison Ice Cave, was a novelty known mostly to Bend residents or deer hunters. It was discovered during a forest fire that swept through the Wanoga Butte area. The Forest Service put a sturdy ladder down into its small circular mouth, but the sands from the adjoining jack pine flats partly filled it in late years.

A couple of early-day ranch hands mentioned other ice caves between Horse Ridge and Frederick Butte. But with their passing, these caves will be forgotten.

Outsiders are fascinated by the pitted lava rock of this interior region. But ranchers who have been wearily plucking each new year's crop off their fields, to pile them in huge rows, must scratch their heads in wonder at seeing truckloads of these go by on Highway 97 on their way to Portland rock gardens.

For many years, the rock fences out-mileaged the barbed wire type. Where the bosom of Mother Earth lies exposed to the sun in the form of bare lava flow, the fence holes are built above ground. A square crib or triangle of juniper posts filled as an anchor every 40 feet or so puts this non-precious material to use.

This lava-lumped landscape added problems to the road builders in the Model T days. To solve that problem on the high desert east of Bend, the future Burns highway was sectioned off so the various inhabitants of this remote region could undertake the dubious job of rolling and scraping rock and grubbing sage to give it the semblance of a road.

The three Stenkamp brothers and the King family built a section to the Harney County line by dragging heavy logs behind teams on the cleared strip.

"It was *cold* that job!" Henry reminisced. "We slept in wagons and froze under a bedroll of four blankets. It took us about three weeks."

Buttes are another novelty of this land. They might be hills any other place, but here they are buttes. Most are cinder cones, timbered on the north and east slopes and sparse of growth on the south and west. (If by "sparse," we mean the devilish manzanita growth.) Lava outcroppings bristle the slopes of others. Several other buttes like Lava, Klawhop, and LeConte Crater, the latter on Wickiup Plain, have fine, large cones in their tops. They are all fine places to gather twisted cinder cones, lava bombs, and dead, bleached manzanita limbs for centerpieces.

The most picturesque part of the butte family history is their names: Pilpil, Kweo, Ooskan, China Hat, Kokostick, Wigtop, Kwinnum, Polytop, Klawhop, Taghum, Ipswoot, Topso, and Lumrum are a start for the unusual names they boast. Others bore pioneer family names such as Firestone, Tetherow, Moffit, and Bates. Yet others had names changed, such as Cat Butte that became Bessie Butte after it was logged. Happy confusion!

Dozens have abandoned lookout towers on them, much used in the early Forest Service days, as the knobs rose 300 to 600 feet above the timbered flatlands.

Brookings Hotel or Half-Way House

Horace and Addie Brookings founded and operated Half-Way House between Bend and Burns in the early 1900's. She was a schoolteacher. Their house became the Hotel at Rolyat and was later Called Brookings Station. Above: to right is Mary McMullin's shack on her claim. (Brookings photos)

Two of Bend's unusually named landmarks were buildings, not buttes. Two early businessmen by the name of Johnson erected frame buildings. One was two stories high, the other three. As the months passed and the men and the buildings were in use, the problem was solved by calling the one man "Two-Story Johnson" and the other man "Three-Story Johnson."

"Brookings Halfway House" on the Burns highway had a practical reference: it was midway between Bend and Burns.

The name "Indian Ford," given to the picnic spot a few miles west of Sisters, was the modern name given to it. Here the Indians camped in later years on their trek to the hopyards in the valley to earn themselves seasonal money. But Mrs. Zumwalt of Sisters and others said that for years before that the little creek was always Slough Creek.

Another name was born when a group of riders chasing wild horses east of Bend saw them apparently disappear in thin air. A closer look revealed three huge caves, one an open tunnel of lava flow with side openings, that these animals had been using for years for shelter from winter winds and summer heat. Thus Horse Caves got its name.

Other names have been around so long that their origins have been lost and forgotten. One such is Powell's Buttes, now called Powell Butte. To this writer, the earliest known account of it was mentioned in *An Illustrated History of Central Oregon:* "Prior to the murderous attacks attending the gold rush to Canyon City, a small detachment of the Hudson's Bay Company was massacred at Powell's Buttes, about eight miles southwest of the present site of the county seat (Prineville) and during many years following . . . there were occasional outbreaks of the savages at which times the whites were mercilessly slaughtered."[1]

Prineville still bears the family name of Barney Prine, its founder and first settler of any consequence in the area. There are a few engaging names to enter into the ledger from that country too: Chicahominy Creek, Hardscrabble Ridge, and Hash Rock add color to the Ochoco sector.

Accounts of the early exploration sometimes gave spellings of place-names considerably different from those seen in today's maps, as in the following:

Aside from Nomadic trappers it is quite probable that the first white men to cross the territory now comprising Crook county were General John C. Fremont and Kit Carson. They explored a section of this country in 1843. The route of this party was as follows: Entering the county at the northwest corner, between the Warm Springs and Shilike Rivers (Shitike Creek), they proceeded southward on the west side of the Des Chutes river, crossing the Matoles (Metolius River) about three to six miles up from its mouth. Thence they continued in a southerly direction, passing about three miles east of the present town of Sisters, crossed Tornello (Tumalo) creek and came to the Des Chutes river near the present site of Bend. They still continued on the west side of this river in

their journey on such until reaching a point about opposite the present postoffice of Lava, when they crossed the Des Chutes and entered the Big Meadows (Paulina Prairie). Continuing their journey southward they passed where Rosland now stands and entered the territory now embraced in Klamath county. About four miles above the town of Bend can be found to this day evidences of the visit of the Fremont party, where there are logs they used in building a causeway.[2]

The ominous Murder's Creek derived its name from the killing of the miners camped there in 1862.

These men were bivouacked under a sheltering rock, sitting at their fire, talking, when four shots and many arrows were loosed. One of the men was killed outright, and four seriously wounded. Two died shortly after, while hidden in the brush. Another crawled to a nearby ranch and died. Only one survived, but he was always sickly thereafter. One of the arrows was found to be poisoned.

The next party that camped there found a gold watch lost in that desperate getaway.

Some pioneer historians were impressed by distance in this vast land:

Interior Oregon . . . contains many interesting landmarks that are familiar to the stockman of that section.... These landmarks are far apart, and in traveling through the country one always finds it necessary to cover the distance between two of them every day. They are usually watering places and it takes a hard day's travel from one to another in most cases and in some cases it requires travel deep into the night. They stand out in the great Oregon "desert" like the beacon lights and guiding points to the mariner at sea.[3]

---

[1] Gertie Sharp, quoted in *An Illustrated History of Central Oregon* (Spokane, Wash.: Western Historical Publishing Co., 1905), p. 702.

[2] Ibid, p. 699.

[3] Ibid, Paul Delaney, quoted p. 1094.

Another reference to a well-known spot was contained in this section of Fremont's diary dated December 16, 1843:

We traveled this morning through snow about three feet deep, which, being crusted, very much cut the feet of our animals. The mountain still gradually rose; we crossed several spring heads covered with quaking asp, otherwise it was all pine forest. The air was dark with falling snow, which everywhere weighed down the trees. The depths of the forest were profoundly still; and below, we scarce felt a breath of the wind which whirled the snow through their branches. I found that it required some exertion of constancy to adhere steadily to one course through the woods, when we were uncertain how far the forest extended, or what lay beyond; and, on account of our animals, it would be bad to spend another night on the mountain. Toward noon the forest looked clear ahead, appearing suddenly to terminate; and beyond a certain point we could see no trees. Riding rapidly ahead to this spot, we found our selves on the verge of a vertical and rocky wall of the mountain. At our feet — more than a thousand feet below — we looked into a green prairie country, in which a beautiful lake, some twenty miles in length, was spread out along the foot of the mountains, its shores bordered with green grass. Just then the sun broke out among the clouds, and illuminated the country below, while around us the storm raged fiercely. Not a particle of ice was to be seen on the lake, or snow on its borders, and all was like summer or spring. The glow of the sun in the valley below brightened up our hearts with sudden pleasure, and we made the woods ring with joyful shouts to those behind; and gradually as each came up, he stopped to enjoy the unexpected scene. Shivering on snow three feet deep, and stiffening in a cold north wind, we exclaimed at once that the names of Summer Lake and Winter Ridge should be applied to these two proximate places of such sudden and violent contrast. [4]

As this inland area was luring settlers, land developers became legion. Mrs. Paul Riedell said, "In 1913 when we came to Bend, it seemed every third building was a land development office."

Tents were strung up so endlessly along the Deschutes in Bend that one lady said it took her three days before she found her relatives camped there.

Mrs. Hethorne recalled, "I paid a locater $25 to take me to our plot, and as usual, he showed us big spuds, supposedly grown there."

Gus Schuman got off the train on arriving, took one look at this upstart town, and asked the station master when the next train was leaving. He had just come from the lush midwest farm country and the contrast was too much.

Forty-four years later, he still hadn't taken that train.

"I had just graduated from an automotive electrical school. I hiked downtown and saw cars sitting everywhere. It was payday at the sawmills and some were having trouble getting their rigs started. I rented a small place at the north end of Wall Street, now Smith Electric, and was up to my ears in work," he said. He spent the weekends hunting and fishing during the next 40 some years.

Charlie Boyd declared, "This country grows on one. I've been here for 60 years and I'm still exploring it." His dad had Bend's first meat-cutting and packing plant.

As Bill Triplett mused, "We knew how to enjoy life then. We lived slower, were happier. If we wanted to go someplace, we didn't think anything of packing up and

---

[4] Quoted in *An Illustrated History of Central Oregon*, pp. 806-807.

Hotel Odell on Odell Lake, 1912. (Kelly photo)

taking three weeks or a month to get our winter's fish and meat. Now people hardly speak to their next-door neighbor."

Some of the land tracts got a small distinction by the name change of ownership. One such was Carrol Acres, of Bend. When money got short, this land was the pot in a particularly hot poker game. The tipster mentioned three of the participants in this game as being Hudsom, Noonchester, and Carrol. Carrol won the pot and Carrol Acres it remains today.

The Millicans homesteaded the Horse Ridge territory for many years. When they left, P. B. Johnson ran a general store at the location of their well. Surprisingly, there was a small seep spring in the area until some cattle plugged it. It was good for three or four pails of water a day. When an attempt was made to dig it and clean it, the water refused to emerge anymore.

That town, Millican, next was a bachelor settlement. It was known as the "one-man town." George Millican was fire chief, mayor, policeman, dogcatcher, and private citizen.

George Millican built his own windmill frame and that picturesque profile was famed all over the high desert. When it started weathering and falling into disrepair, he ordered a steel successor, but the neighbors raised so much hob with the idea that George worked it over once more to put it back into use while the new steel sections lay gathering

Millican Landmark

dust.

Pictures of this memorable landmark are scarce, and those possessing one cherish it.

Today in that country, the wild horses are not "raising their dusts" anymore, as former cowpoke Bill Pyatt so aptly put it. Most of all the shacks have fallen and the bustling homesteads have been stilled by time. The wheezing pumps have drawn their last drink of water.

Because there was just so much dying a man could do, so many days of defeat he could take, he watched his last desert sunset, then moved to town. He had gotten his baptism by fire.

Yet, the desert has a mystique all its own. Even today, someone is always searching the desert. What are they looking for? Is it peace? Tranquility? Clean air? Serenity? Time? All these are here, and more, if they look and listen closely.

To learn how far removed we are from those years comes as a shock.

A while back, Jack Eby and Bob Joanis took several explorer scouts out on the desert to poke around for agate, Indian points, and petrified wood. They camped out for the night in a line cabin on the G. I. Ranch. It had the usual wood range in it.

The teenage youths had their first look at this wonderful contraption and were completely fascinated by it. The exploring was forgotten as they experimented with its various dampers and openings. They filled it with wood, coddled it, pestered and poked the fire, and generally smoked everyone out of the shack. Then they asked, "How much do these cost? We want one!"

And there are other items that this generation would puzzle over that once held a prominent place in a kitchen, pantry, or barn. Apple peelers, hog scrapers, corn shellers, candle molds, shotshell loaders, matchholders are all a holdover from those dusty days. And those who would recognize them in an instant would enter themselves in the ledgers as pioneers.

Prineville still has its share of houses resplendent with gingerbread decorations: faded red brick chimneys, bulged fashionably at the top, steep-pitched, four-sided roofs suddenly bristling with short iron grillwork. A look inside would reveal a double-wind Ansonia mantel clock above a tired, creaking rocker, handcarved from stem to stern — of

Frank Ireland and family in 1890's. Central Oregon location unknown. (Al Moore photo)

Lonely Chapman homestead in Fremont, Oregon, 1909. (Walters photo)

Mr. and Mrs. Bert Meeks with children Gladys and Hubert, 1910, at their homestead. (Gladys Workman)

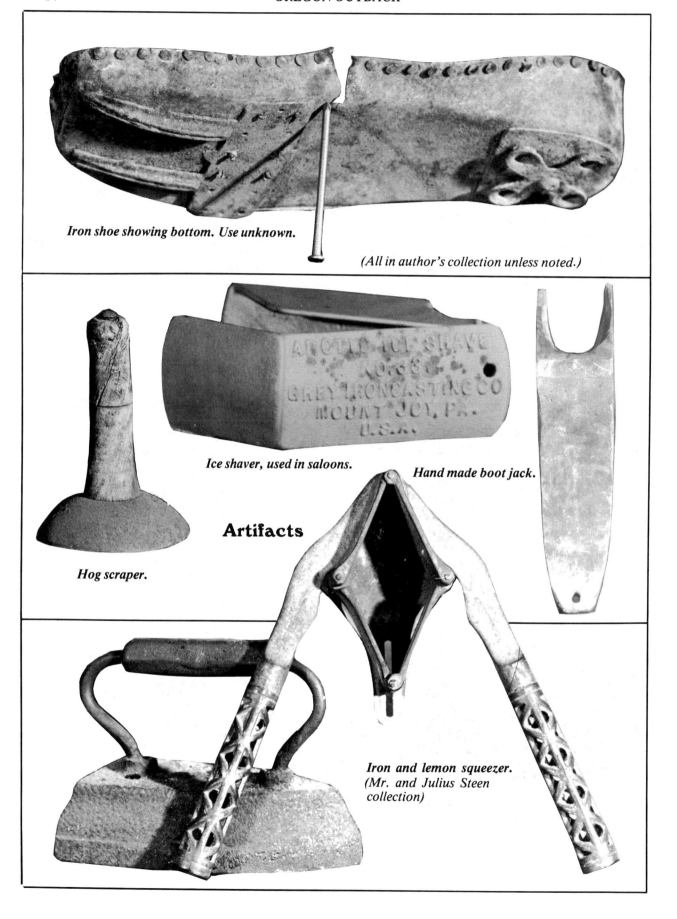

Iron shoe showing bottom. Use unknown.

(All in author's collection unless noted.)

Ice shaver, used in saloons.

Hand made boot jack.

Hog scraper.

Artifacts

Iron and lemon squeezer. (Mr. and Julius Steen collection)

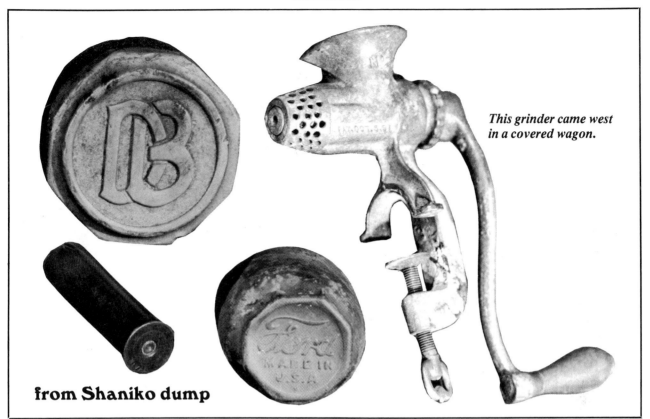

This grinder came west in a covered wagon.

from Shaniko dump

course, the old man's chair.

A wise man once said, "He who owns the soil, owns to the sky."

These settlers felt this. Merchant, trapper, farmer, cowpoke, teacher, mechanic, all at some time past owned a corner of this land. They felt it in the few sunny days of spring, when starts of cabbage plants sat in the south window. They felt it in summer when rye stood to their waist, and again in the fall when a crosscut sang out and juniper chunks fell, one by one. They felt it in the bitter winter, when cold pressed to the earth with every fibre of its being, and the mountains had been dusted overnight with their ermine finery.

The rawboned lumberjacks, of saw and snoose and steel-whipped lines, had their corner of it, in the stifling green of summer and the naked beauty of winter. The leaded gray sky, a curve of snow, and the liquid black of a brook was the setting for their winter workshop. All of them built the land and took away from it. The land built them and took away from them. The land hasn't changed much, but the generations have.

Now people have inside plumbing in a camper instead of a tent that flaps like some contented, peaceful thing. They fish with a spinning outfit, not a bamboo pole. They want a 50-horse inboard where some used to use oars. They languish in front of a color TV instead of attending the once endless whirl of dances, card parties, and socials. They turn up the heat with a thermostat and grow a potbelly, while the crosscut saw hangs like a novelty on the front yard fence.

The only thing that keeps us from further receding from a close touch with this earth is our increasing leisure time. When time hangs heavy enough on the hands of the new generations, they too will take to the fields, foothills, and dry washes, and rediscover this same land.

Then there will be something to recapture, as when the old-timers sat on the porch watching a sunset laced with fire, or heard the aspens whispering of storms to come. Perhaps once again, the plaintive notes of a mouth organ will die on the desert vastness. And they will hear the wind at night, with a sob in its throat, banging a tattered screen door.

They felt it, and loved it, and reveled in it, because this was their land.

CHAPTER 3

Things Petrified

When the settlers were through grubbing sage, planting crops, and building fences, they took time off to ride to the streams and hills and woods and desert to relax and explore. It didn't take them long in piecing a small find here and a major one there to learn that Oregon was richly endowed with agate, fossils, geodes, thunder eggs, and things petrified.

Lay a map of the state out in front of you. Start marking in the area north at Biggs Junction and head southeast through Grass Valley, Willowdale, Ashwood, Prineville, Mitchell, Paulina, Brothers, Glass Buttes, Wagontire, Burns, Stinkingwater, Harper, and on to the wild Owyhee. These landmarks and towns roughly encompass a wide swath through Oregon that is rich in agate, jasper, amethyst, carnelian, and related semi-precious stones.

Treasured bits of palm root, figs, dates — either opalized or agatized, all potential conversation pieces — sit in prominent places in Oregon homes. Fossilized snakes, fire opal, jasper in ton chunks, pressed-leaf prints in rock, and petrified woods in myriad colors lie half-hidden in dry washes until a sharp-eyed rock hound spots them.

Lava bombs, the egg-shaped core of cinder clinkers spewed up from volcanic action, are found on many of the butte tops.

Oregon diamonds are found on Wagontire Mountain. They are clear, pastel-shaded gems having blue, green, pink, or amber tints. They polish up to make fine stones for rings and other jewelry.

The agatized woods abound in color, red to green, slinky black, spooky grays, pink and clear, white-plumed, blue with dendrites, orange, yellow, ad infinitum.

Back in the sixties, there was a big to-do

Surprising Things Petrify

Several years back, Mr. Mosley told of a large petrified man they plowed up while living on their homestead in the Ashwood country. He was a nuisance — too heavy to load, too dead to walk, and too large to roll out of the way. In the ensuing years, just when they were getting used to him, he started breaking up.

The Mosleys were too busy coaxing a living from the inhospitable ground to take trips of a scientific nature by horse and wagon to either of Oregon's universities.

Treasures are lost in simple ways. The stone man was probably worth a fortune.

---

over the Cougar Mountain Cave discovery of woven sandals of juniper bark that carbon-dated to several thousand years old. Why all the fuss? The hooky-playing boys attending the Young School east of Bend scooped this important find by many years. Roughly a quarter-mile east of the school, on Dr. Cutter's property, is a large cave, quite hidden in the junipers. Some of the boys who skipped school explored it from time to time and brought home woven sandals, fine obsidian knives and tools, and various other points found in the sand of the cave floor. Because of their surreptitious activities, their finds were not broadcast as they might have been. This was in the thirties.

Thunder eggs were recently made Oregon's official state rock. These stones are generally round, rough or pebbled with lumps on their matrix or surface, the outer coating of color varying from the localities where they are found. They come in browns, tans, greens and grays and chalky whites. Any rock hound worth his salt can tell pretty closely what part of the state an egg came from just by the color of its matrix. The size of the eggs varies from that of a filbert or walnut to a basketball.

The rock hound cuts into them with varying emotions — no two are alike. Mrs. Jolley of Bend has one with gold in its center. Some have crystals in varying colors, or moss, plumes or bushes, bands, tubes, iris or iridescent qualities, and vivid colors of every hue.

The Jolleys also had some eggs that gurgled when shaken, so out of curiosity, they had some of them cut in half with a diamond saw. The eggs were nothing unusual in color nor worth polishing, but they had a peculiar, thick, clear liquid in their centers. The halves, moistened from the spilled liquid, were slapped together where they held by adhesion of the mysterious contents.

Some months later, the talk got around to the Jolleys' unusual watery thunder eggs. After rummaging around in dozens of boxes of rocks, they were brought out. The beholders were bewildered to see the once-halved sections now completely cemented together again. The cut surfaces, somewhat offset when slapped together, were now solid and indistinguishable from the original matrix. The halves, once wet with that mysterious liquid, were now whole, brittle and hard as the other uncut eggs.

The petrified plum, mentioned earlier, is registered and catalogued by the Smithsonian Institution. It is quite translucent and a twin in color for any Royal Ann cherry, freshly picked.

The petrified, or fossilized, snake, is about 14 inches long, black and mottled, and partially coiled. It was found among some rocks in the Paulina area.

Another amateur geologist has a fossil of a dried frog.

Locations of some of the other geological goodies are off limits to the white man because of their being on the Warm Springs Indian Reservation. Beautifully clear chunks of crystal as well as thunder eggs of good quality have been found there.

The "beds" of eggs are invariably found near water of some sort, whether a spring, a creek, or whatever or else there is evidence of water's having once been there in the far past.

Prineville, in 1904, had its share of saloons, but Smith's, about a block south of the present traffic light, did a booming business for several weeks as a result of a peculiar find. Walt McCoin told the story, recalling Emmet White and two other men almost breaking up the party with an occupant they carried into Smith's back room one night.

Their prize was a small-to-average-sized petrified man. Walt said that after a lengthy discussion by the sober and partly sober, they decided the stone man was an Indian. A scar on its chest resembled a stab wound, and parts of three fingers on one hand had broken off from the rough wagon ride. Walt recalls the men were heading south, toward California, with their prize.

A similar story is told in a published book:

In 1920 Watts came to the Hay Creek Cemetery with Mrs. McPherson to move the body of her daughter to The Dalles to be reburied by the side of her father. The young lady had been buried at Hay Creek for six years and great difficulty was experienced in digging, as the soil is similar to that in the Burns Cemetery, very hard to dig, but pulverizing when exposed to air. The outside box and coffin had completely rotted away. This made digging more difficult and as Watts carefully lifted the body he was astonished to find it petrified. It was a new experience, so with interest he noted the darker hue the skin had taken on, resembling leather. He considered this the only perfect work of sculpture he had ever seen. The trip to The Dalles was a nightmare of fear, lest the body break. The body of stone was wrapped in a blanket and placed in the back of the pickup on a board. As he bounced over the rough roads he could hear the body rattle and he was sure that the fingers and toes would

McCoins, Homesteaders at Gray Butte

McCoin homestead at Gray Butte. McCoins buckarooed and raised cattle for 60 years in Central Oregon. The last drive was in the early 1960's. (McCoin photo)

Julius and Sara McCoin, homesteaders in the 1880's where Haystack Dam is now. Their son, Walt saw the petrified man. (McCoin photo)

McCoins, Montgomerys and Messingers in the Haystack area. (McCoin photo)

Walter McCoin, pioneer cowboy.

He ran wild horses at the turn of the century at Willow Creek Basin, later called Palmain and finally, Madras. He saw the petrified man at Smith's Saloon in Prineville in 1904. (McCoin photo)

be broken off, but when he reached The Dalles he was relieved to find his fears were groundless.[1]

No account of Oregon's colorful rock country would be complete without mentioning the ammunition dumps of the early-day Indians for their tools and weapons. These were the natural glass or obsidian outcroppings and deposits found in this high plateau country. The most fabled location lies between the twin lake nestled in Newberry Crater. Other sources include Quartz Mountain, Dry Butte, Glass Buttes, and many places in the environs of Burns.

The dusky artisans used chalcedony, flint, agate, and jasper as well as several types of chert for their tools and points.

This "natural black glass" many times is not just that — it is striped with gray, brown, or red. There are other types that, when cut in thin slices and held to the light, have the look of billowing curtains or drapes flowing in natural folds. Flecks of gold sheen show in other cuts.

The Indian work on points in the northwest country is said by some authorities to be among the finest in North America. Fort Rock, Christmas Valley, and Silver Lake areas were fine places to search out points. But the United States government, in its infinite wisdom, has forbidden the picking up of any points. That law will be about as hard to enforce as Prohibition was. These areas were so rich in points because our dusky cousins knew that the mule deer wintered there in immense numbers.

Ranchers in the area found many Indian bowls, some so large they had to leave them. These are variously called metates, squaw kitchens, or bread boards. Enterprising ranchers used many for their gate posts to pivot in.

The Walt McCoins of Terrebonne were involved in another type of petrified tale which occurred at their onetime ranch at the edge of the Crooked River Gorge, near Highway 97.

About 1933, they were making some changes in corrals and fences. One tree, about 14 inches through, was cut off to use as a gate post. They had a lot of trouble cutting it, since the outer surface was unusually hard; it could not even be nicked with a knife, and, still later, staples could not be driven into it. Yet the center portion was soft enough to probe with a sharp instrument.

It was slowly petrifying from the outside in.

In the same area, east of the highway bridge along the north rim, once ran a river, ages ago. Geologic changes opened the canyon so the river is now 400 feet lower. But topside, pieces of agate and petrified wood, washed many centuries by an unknown river, have rounded ends, smoothed from the water's action.

A petrified girl, a fossilized Indian, an agatizing tree, a stone man too huge to move, and some mysterious liquid cementing thunger eggs — all these in a matter of months or years seem to indicate that, in our smugness, we should reassess our ideas on the petrifying process. Heretofore we had thought the time involved in such creations took millenia. Yet here we have examples involving incredibly short periods, geologically speaking.

This is a fascinating land. Any trip, innocently started, could well lead to intriguing discoveries. Get yourself a rock hammer, a dry wash, a pair of stout legs and sharp eyes, and you are in the business of geology and archaeology in the same breath.

Nature still teaches us in the timeless language of the universe, if we would but listen. There is some of the archaeologist in all of us. Why else do we scavenge in the dump heaps of yesteryear to return delightedly with an artifact from another age? We are much like the cunning workers of obsidian and bone, covered by the thin veneer of civilization, removed from that time by only a few shadowy generations.

---

[1] Evada R. Power, "Hay Creek," in *Jefferson County Reminiscences,* (Portland, Or.: Binfords & Mort, 1957), p. 33.

CHAPTER 4

Crops, Weather, and Such

Mrs. Thom, who spent many years in the Silver Lake area with her husband, Dr. Thom, once quipped that they could grow everything but bananas in that part of the state. Others who have tried gardening for a hobby in the Bend sector, and had their tidbits frosted every month during the summer, are of a different turn of mind.

Somewhere in between these two weather outposts lies an area in which the ranchers plant in the cold month of May, then trust to the Almighty that they may harvest in the heady weather of September.

That they are not millionaires from their efforts or crops is a well-known fact. But the valleys in and around Prineville, the irrigated lands of Culver and Madras, and the farm plots lying at the base of the Powell Butte hills give enough of a return from labors that the communities are generally prosperous.

Mint has replaced certified clover seed in fields the Bureau of Reclamation ditches irrigate.

Why some enterprising grower doesn't try sugar beets here is a mystery. Many are reluctant to try new crops, although onions grown for seed are a newcomer lately.

The early Pilgrim ranchers, with high hopes, lots of ambition, and lean pocket books planned on making fortunes in wheat. They settled on rye, barley, and oats for the most part. Until the drought of the early thirties came and clung tenaciously to the land, Metolius shipped tons of hard wheat, famed even to the midwest for its quality. That hamlet boasted its own bank, mainly from the profits of that wheat. In speaking of rye, Karl Kleinfeldt said, "One year, rye was so high that a man could walk 20 feet into it and disappear."

A settler in the Fork Rock vicinity told how

their family grubbed 80 acres by hand and planted wheat. The first few years, they got two to three ton to the acre, but the yield got gradually poorer. The year that they switched to rye was 1917.

Except for areas well-protected from the ever-prevalent frost, fruit has a discouraging yield, unless it is of the berry variety. But during that crucial period when the blooms are on, and the frost holds off, about one in five or six years, there is such a flood of apples, pears, and plums — even a few peach and apricot trees — that much of the fruit can't be given away.

Tomatoes, cucumbers, corn, and zucchini grow quite regularly in Redmond, Terrebonne, Culver, Madras, and Prineville, but the greenhouses are a safer bet for Bend and Burns. Surprisingly, though, a lady whose family homesteaded in the early-day Squaw Creek-Grandview sector grew corn, ground cherries, peanuts, apricots, and apples for themselves and the Huntingtons, Zumwalts, and others settling there.

One hundred sacks of certified clover seed from fields west of Tumalo. 1930's. (Ted Becker photo)

Though much of this soil is light, sandy, and heavy (percentage-wise) with pumice, the alfalfa grown here is highly sought after by the dairy and cattlemen of the Willamette Valley. It is a common thing to see dozens of semi's trucking the high protein hay over the Cascades every fall.

With so much frost and cold out of season in this inland plateau, the honied taste of spring didn't lay sweetly over the land, but it was inevitable that some of this did pay off.

Such was the case one March when Mr. Boyd was running out of ice for his meat plant, the first of its kind in Bend. A prolonged warm spell had pressured him so badly that he was almost out of the coolant. He couldn't close down operations to take a team for the three-day trip to Arnold Ice Cave southeast of town. It was one day out, one there, cutting and loading, and one back, by team.

Then a cold snap hit, of zero weather, and froze ice ten inches deep on Swalley Pond, the close-in source of it. The spell lasted for three days running. This was the spring of 1911.

When it wasn't frost, the Gray Butte settlers found aphids killing young fruit trees they had been babying for months. Quite by

Louis Hill of Powell Butte checking grain in 1910. He was the brother of James Day Hill, the railroad magnate. (Kelly photo)

Silver Lake threshing crew, 1899. (Earl Small)

The town of Brothers on the high desert. (Brookings photo)

chance, the youngsters solved the problem by telling folks about the millions of ladybugs they had seen on the very top of the butte under rocks there one spring. The oldsters put two and two together and went for a look for themsleves. Thereafter, annual pilgrimages were made each spring up the ancient hill to fill pails with the beneficial insects to war on the leaf pests. And someone — no one remembers who — started a pillar of flat rocks that grew higher with each succeeding trip. Long after ladybugs weren't needed, that landmark was visible to travelers coming east from Camp Polk. It stood for years as a kind of memorial to pioneers, long since departed.

Then one day, in the 1940's, Mrs. Helfrich saw through her window a bunch of young bucks climbing the great hill. It had been years since anyone had, so she watched through binoculars with curiosity. But curiosity turned to dismay when she saw them tear down the old pillar that so many hands of the various pioneers had built, to scatter it down the bare flanks of the peak. It was never rebuilt.

Southeast of Gray Butte, near Brothers, a transplanted Canadian had just moved in to settle anew. He was Mr. Goodman, a Jewish man of the soil who had had much luck in farming elsewhere. The month was June, and things looked good for finally setting his roots, but the bright song of spring changed all that. It clouded up, turned suddenly cold, and in the next half hour snowed two inches. Mr. Goodman took one long look, loaded his belongings in his two-wheeled wagon, and delivered this parting shot at a watching neighbor: "T'hell with this country! I'm back to Canada where it doesn't snow all summer!"

Any central or eastern Oregonian will tell you it should have been "back to the drawing board" when the good Lord drew up His plans for their springs. They are unlike any normal spring. Snows in June and July send campers scurrying for home from the high lakes every few years. Shorts and halters are standby vacation duds; here they are backed up with long johns.

Dave Cody, who spent half a century just north of Brothers, recalled another June 22 when it snowed eight inches. The year is forgotten, but the event remembered when the grain crops were all lodged from the weight of another June snow.

In 1963, I believe it was, one inch of snow fell in the Lost Forest, making the return trip from there a nightmare for this writer's family on a point-hunting trip; the road was a quagmire.

From some of the aforegoing, it might be assumed that farming in sections of this dry side of the state is a sketchy business. It is true.

But we must report the fabulous with the failures. Henry Stenkamp in the Brothers area had such a bumper crop of rutabagas and turnips one late fall that he sold his produce for a mere $5 a wagonload. Some of the whoppers were as big as a stovepipe section and weighed as much as 18 pounds apiece.

Another retired pioneer, now living in Bend, remembered seeing a 91-pound pumpkin grown on the Redmond experimental plot when it was first started.

The Hugh Dugans, living north of Pilot Butte in a relatively frost-free belt, got two cotton plants from relatives one spring. By careful and patient nursing on the southern exposure of their house, they triumphantly harvested two cotton bolls that fall. No, they didn't corner the cotton market.

Junipers: 600 to 2,000 Years Old

Before we look down our nose at junipers, however we must recognize a single, ennobling quality in all of them. They will grow and thrive in lands where no other tree can survive. They are disheveled, bedraggled, and commonplace. They are the comics of the tree world, the Charlie Chaplin of the evergreens. But like that comic, they have a dignity with their dishevelment and character in their chaos.

Like all young plants, the juniper seedlings need shade and protection from extremes in weather. And that young sprout boasts a blue rarely seen in nature, a pale, dry, dusty, powder blue. They are prickly, to discourage the deer and antelope. But the adult tree dislikes shade and seems to thrive in the pitiless desert sun.

Juniper wood is incredibly tough. A juniper tree will take abuse that would kill most any other kind. A walk through that land reveals scars, wind breaks, stubs of limbs, lightning strikes, barbed wire loops, and many other tortures man and nature has inflicted, and still the trees live. That junipers are very tenacious of life is proved by their age. They are among the oldest living things on the North American continent. Estimates of their age vary from 600 years to 2000 years. But these estimates are just that — estimates. Their age is conjecture, because of the all-prevalent heartwood white-pocket rot that eats the inner trunk and the large limbs. Growth lines per inch run from 30 to 80.

Emil Van Lake remarked, "I cut one red juniper off a rocky ridge that was solid and six feet through. This one tree furnished us with wood all one winter."

In northern Lake County, just a little west of Buzzard Rock, rises what was for years thought to be Oregon's largest juniper. Coyotes came from miles around, and proud they were to lift their legs against such a venerable giant. Then a party of three discovered and measured a larger specimen in the Lost Forest.

From the foot of the Cascades to Redmond, then east to Horse Ridge, and again southeast, the sea of junipers reaches forth in a grand array seen nowhere else on earth.

There are few conditions that will kill these trees or that they cannot adapt to. Mistletoe growth, a parasite much like the oak's, will over a long period kill them. Too much water will do it occasionally — this occurs when new homes are built in the arid juniper groves where the trees are used to aridity. Then, a prolonged period of heavy watering or irrigating before their root system can adapt to it will do in some of the older trees.

Numerous livestock pastured in a confined area will rub the trees bare of bark so they will die in a year or two. Two-by-fours nailed vertically around the trunks will stop this.

Juniper wood resembles cedar in look and smell. It is highly prized by woodworkers for turning bowls, candlesticks, and figures. It takes a satin finish, with a background of red, brown, or black streaks patterning the grain.

The tree in shape, texture, contour, and growth mimics dozens of other trees; the droop of the weeping willow, the bulk of the oak, the slender beauty of ornamental evergreens are found in their number. The limbs spiral clockwise and counterclockwise. Some are flat and palmated and spiraled. Other specimens are huge, bushlike trees, with many trunks sweeping to tops of 20 feet across.

The growth in some trees is so dense as to form globs of almost inpenetrable growth. Juniper mistletoe is delicate, fragile, and pink, but still a good substitute here in season.

Deer feeding on certain of these trees add an unsolved riddle to be investigated. In the mule deer wintering grounds of the Fort Rock sector are trees that are eaten clean as high as they can be reached. Why these, when thousands of others remain untouched? Is it that each tree has an individual taste of its own much as the delicate differences noted in each separate strawberry or raspberry? Yet after the deer move to the timber and mountain lands in the spring, and this growth has a chance to return to these trees in succeeding seasons, they are seldom if ever touched again as food.

Other years, 16-foot sunflowers have been raised here. Yet Mr. Kleinfeldt ruefully recalled his spud-raising with this comment: "When I tried some years, the frost bit them, the jacks ate them, the wild horses ran through them, and the cottontails dug them up."

Like the domestic garden crops, the native plants are not of the spectacular variety, either in number or type. Juniper, sage and rabbit brush, bunchgrass, bitter brush, coyote berry, and mountain mahogany constitute the menu for most of the desert. Of these, the bunchgrass and bitter brush made the cattlemen prosper and the sheep men thrive. The junipers didn't do much for anyone, except heat their shacks and hold their barbed wire.

Mountain mahogany is another desert plant found on certain high ridges and buttes. It is a favorite food of mule deer in the fall. But, again, studies made in Colorado show that in a short period of a day or two, the animals will turn to this plant or others for feed, and then leave them just as quickly at certain periods. Is it a chemical change that frost triggers in the plants?

The manzanita and snowbrush of the cut-over yellow pine country are two other individuals that rate a description.

Manzanita, the Johnny-come-lately, springs up after logging operations in this ponderosa pine belt. The plant is a delight to wildlife and a curse to man. The limbs of the brush are red-barked, twisted, and tough; the damage they can do to a deer hunter's clothes in a short journey through it for the fetching of a buck is appalling. The deer eat the shoots, the mice and bird nest in its growth or roots and feed on its fruit. Bears also feed on it in the late summer. Its growth is a blessing to the foothills in preventing erosion. Its waxy, green leaves, as well as the snow brush, are a joy against winter snows.

To take on these two plants in combat by a walk through them is like facing the ranks of bowmen and lancers. Few mule deer hunters will, but those that do, with the smug knowledge of what they are doing, generally score on a craggy buck.

Sugar pine trees are interspersed among yellow pine stands, but are highly selective of altitude, topography, and rainfall amounts it seems, as the stands are scarce. The cones lure many city dwellers to secret and remote areas, known only to themselves, every autumn or so. They are prized because of their surprising length, which often reaches 16 to 18 inches. When sprayed, gilded, and bedecked with spangles and sparkle, they make most unusual Christmas gifts for friends in the more prosaic sections of the United States, like the midwest of east. The Indians used the seeds for food.

That about covers the greenery of this semi-desert land. Though our western river valleys have a lush growth, ours is crabbed and slow. And while our weather is always a wedge for starting small talk, year in and year out, we have an incredible number of sunny days per year. We compare favorably with Arizona in this respect. And, happily, the nights are cool. Blankets are year-round fare.

Stimulating as the weather is, it is kind to things being weathered. Things don't rot here, they age.

For boards, timbers, and fence posts, there is a drying out, a gathering of character from moss and lichens. It is then that drab orange, bright green, and flaked gray cover wood and rock with the quiet beauty of weathering.

All this belies that classic remark dropped by one veteran of many seasons: "If there is something nice about central Oregon springs, I haven't been here long enough to discover what it is yet."

CHAPTER 5

Not Quite Supermarkets

The old general store was a melange of odors, supplies, and commodities seldom to be seen today. Open-barreled goodies and homespun philosophy from the always occupied chairs have been replaced by cold efficiency and shotgun checking aisles.

Up into the middle sixties, central Oregon had at least one store that still retained that delightful mixture of smells to take one across the threshold of yesterday's stores — 50 years at one bound. The general store in the town of Metolius slips one into the time machine of not quite supermarkets.

The slick adman of today would consider some of yesterday's advertising pretty wild stuff. For example: "Ordinary flour will only make from 270 to 280 loaves of bread to the barrel. *White River Flour* is guaranteed to make 300 loaves; therefore, at 5¢ a loaf, White River Flour is worth $1.50 per barrel more than ordinary lower-priced flour." This was fact. It was in the Lynch and Roberts catalogue of May 1916. So a housewife had to know her arithmetic as well as her cooking.

To let this inland world know where to get such bargains, two up-and-coming grocers, M. A. Lynch and J. R. Roberts of Redmond, had a large sign painted on immense basalt-slabbed walls of the Crooked River Gorge where the stages had to wind their way down the precipitous north wall passage. Both that sign, and another on a large boulder at Lower Bridge of the Deschutes River crossing, are still visible. The latter is the crossing to forgotten Camp Polk and on to the valley.

All travelers going that route got the "hard sell" through basalt advertising.

The partners started their store in 1912 in Redmond. Laras and Sathers were in Bend a little earlier, about 1904.

Products, familiar now, were listed then in that musty catalogue, and were old names even at that time. Among them were Jell-O, Roman Meal, Royal Baking Powder, Albers Oats, Puffed Wheat and Puffed Rice, Cream of Wheat, Gold Dust, Lea and Perrins Sauce, Heinz Catsup, and Knox Sparkling Gelatine.

This was before the day of cancer sticks and smoking habits have changed so much that only a few will recognize some of the following brands that were sold in those misty days of yore: Bagley's Sweet Tips, Bull Durham, City Club, Corn Cake, Dixie Queen, Duke's Mixture, Edgeworth R. R., Geo. Washington, Gold Shore, Lucky Strike, Maryland Club, Matoaka, Patterson's Seal, Peerless, Pedro, Qboid, Stag, Tuxedo, Twin Oaks Mixture, Velvet and the inevitable Prince Albert. A brand called Satisfaction Cut Plug even offered a bonus: "Buy it and get a 16 oz. lunch box with hinged top and handle."

These were all pipe tobaccos. The four standby chewing tobaccos were Star, Horse Shoe, Climax, and Piper Heidsick.

If the inflation spiral has your ulcers churning, settle down with these prices. Pearl Top lamp chimneys were only $1.45 a dozen. A fine, galvanized gallon oil can was a mere two bits. Candies were also a quarter— for a dozen. Crackers were a dime a box, and baking powder sold for 25¢ for half a pound!

A lady's rustproof corset was $1 for the economy item to $3 for the deluxe. Men's suits started at $10.50, but B.V.D.'s don't seem like much of a steal at one dollar a suit in those days.

Your courting came cheap: five pounds of chocolates was $1.

Ball mason jars, quart size, were 75¢ a dozen.

An item that most people wouldn't know how to use today, stove blacking, was a dime a cake.

The cheese cutter was set for 5¢ and 10¢ cuts. Tobacco was the same (but with a different cutter).

"Yes, we take cord wood for pay on your bill."

"No! Two-foot lengths, and *piled in the back shed*!"

J. C. Rush founded the town of Lamonta, N.E. of Redmond. He had a store there. (McCoin photo)

Looking North on Wall Street in Bend in 1911. The first break in the wooden buildings at the right is Minnesota Avenue. (Slick Raper photo)

Mannheimers of Bend sold calicos at 5¢ a yard, batiste at 13½¢, and fine silks at 43¢ a yard. Estimating three yards for a dress, milady could have a handmade creation in silk, no less, for $2.

A July 3, 1912, paper listed corn flakes, three packages for a quarter, and soda at four for a quarter. Coffee was just being packaged in cans, steel-cut, and sold at three pounds for a dollar.

For you bottle buffs, the Patterson Drug Company was in business in Bend in 1911. Their ad was in a paper of that date.

Just below that ad was a news item covering the automobile census: "There are 39 autos in Bend in 1912."

Even the "moom pichurs" were getting their licks in with this: "We have the finest in cinemas. Our features are morally good."

Other ad spreads covered different products:

FAREWELL BEND SALOON

Severt Debing, Prop.

Choice Brands of Beer, Wines, Liquors . . . .
Cigars always on hand.

HEADQUARTERS FOR TOURISTS AND TIMBERMEN

Farewell Bend, Oregon

Sometimes a cowpoke, under the influence, rode on into the stores, horse and all. The oil-soaked fir flooring seldom held such weight, so they were pleased when you hitched your mount to the hitching post or rings.

Orders came large for outfits that only got into town twice a year. Three sweaty, dirty cowhands rode into Redmond at 5 p.m. one Saturday with an order that took until 7 p.m. to write up and until Sunday noon (they didn't work Sundays) to fill. The outfit left with six wagons and 18 horses staggering out with 13 tons of supplies.

J. R. Roberts told of another time when he got 100 crates of strawberries in from White Salmon, Washington. He tied 50 of them on an old Reo touring car, on seats and running boards, and headed out for the Paulina-Post country. "They were all out on a rabbit drive when I got near Suplee," he said, "but when I found where they were, I sold the works in 15 minutes. There weren't enough strawberries to go around and they pleaded with me to bring more. The following week, I repeated with another 50." He also recalled an order coming in from a ranch to the east for one ton of bacon.

Mr. Roberts continued, "In 1913, Mrs. Ritter came into the store, looked around, and told us we didn't know how to run the women's department. She talked us into sending out printed invites and ordering 500 carnations. Then she filled the window with new hats.

"About noon, a few days later, the country editor of *The Oregonian* was sitting across the street and wanted to know what all the commotion was. He never saw so many women!"

All of the Sather children worked their hitch in the family's store, and some had vivid memories of some of the rituals.

"I was always carrying in pails of water," one of the boys said, in remembering his chores. "We plucked sprouts from the eyes of potatoes, weighed and sacked sugar, cornmeal and beans. We filled gallon cans of

Main Street, Laidlaw, 1910. Ted Becker photo)

kerosene from the larger five-gallon ones.''

All stores used the package clamp for the stuff on top shelves. Some had a classy arrangement for a moveable ladder on a track.

Another of the Sathers remembered, ''In waiting on the Indian trade, we learned in a hurry never to take anything *out* of a sack once it was poured in. They immediately thought they were being cheated. Pour slowly until the weight was right, with nothing out, and everybody was happy.''

The transient Indians traded fresh huckleberries for supplies, and sold their buckskin handicraft of gloves and moccasins.

Many products were sold from the now defunct Bend Flour Mill. It was the only mill, many oldsters recalled, that sold rye flakes for cooking into cereal.

In the store trade mentioned, little or no small change was used. Whenever possible, items were sold exactly to the quarter, half-dollar, or dollar.

A common practice then was buying what produce they could from local people as crops were in season. While many families peddled milk house to house to earn extra silver, some sold to the stores. The Murk girls, of Laidlaw, used their wooden wagon to deliver, dipping out what the customer wanted. Prices varied from 7¢ to 10¢ a quart, delivered.

The Boyd youngsters, of Bend's Boyd Acres, still recall the running feud their dog, King, had with a neighbor canine on their milk route. The kids had a hardwood wagon with rack and harness for their rounds. But whenever they neared a certain neighborhood, there was chaos in the milk department as the two dogs tangled. Kids were crying — over spilt milk, naturally. King had to be muzzled while the other fighter was not. So a battle strategy was devised.

As they neared the house on the next round, the muzzle was slipped off and one aitch of a fight filled the morning air. When the dust cleared, King was king in fact as well as in name. The milk came through on time from then on.

Some 50 miles south of Bend, in the low desert, there was another country store in business, picking up customers from surrounding homesteaders. In 1910, when word of Halley's comet was all the talk, the storekeeper ordered three wagonloads of coffins because "it was going to sweep all the people off the earth." For years afterward, the trappings of these — hinges and ornate handles — lay scattered in the dust where the store had once stood.

The 1964 Christmas flood washed loose another bit of history on the Claude Vandevert Ranch, on Little River. A bottle was washed free of years of burial bearing the embossed lettering:

Reception Soda Works — Prineville Oregon

We have but a diminished perspective of that time now. The disinherited ranches stand bare. Weekend bottle hounds seek them and rusting remnants of that period. The desert is kind to labels and tin cans in this country and some finds are well preserved.

So they search on, amateur archaeologists, preserving a page of provincial history by digging the dump heaps of another age.

1914 in La Pine. (Slick Raper photo)

CHAPTER 6

Railroads

When the rails were being laid in the race to reach Bend in 1911 and 1912, the 320-foot-deep Crooked River Gorge stopped construction temporarily. The bridge, when finished, was the highest of its kind in the entire United States.

In its building, two crews worked from each side of the rock-ribbed gorge putting up girders and laying track, closing the gap from the north and south rims. The Trail Crossing to the east routed the steel to the south rim where it was stockpiled. When there was only a girder's length or so between each rim, a plank about 3 x 12 was put across between the steel, and the hard-bitten crewmen used that for shuttling material over that awesome thread of river far, far below.

One of the women, the wife of a cook, won a ten dollar bet by crossing that flimsy plank, much to the wonder of these men. A rare courage? No. It was rumored she wanted the $10 for two new hats she saw in Redmond.

In those last days, before reaching Bend, which was the terminal point for the rails, Grover Caldwell kept beef on the tin plates of the crews in that last 15-to-20-mile stretch.

W.D. Cheney, in *The Bend Book*, published in 1911, stated that an average of about two miles of track could be laid per day when the blasting of lava cuts was already done ahead of the crews.[1]

We must have been some plum in those days. At various times, rails were being built or planned to be built from each point of the compass to reach this growing young burg.

Harriman and Hill crews were fighting tooth and nail to reach here first. The Corvallis-Eastern was being pushed from the valley. It had advanced to the point where the

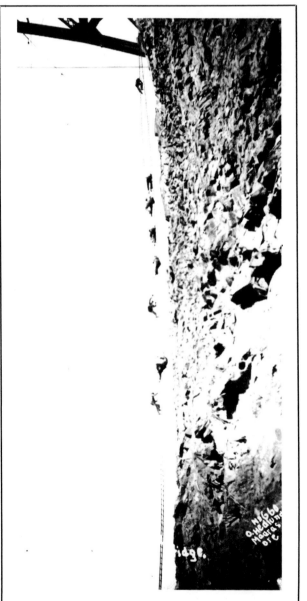

Men climbing 380 feet down rope ladder to bottom of Crooked River Gorge to get material for bridge building. (Kelley photo)

---

[1] W. D. Cheney, *The Bend Book* (Bend Park Company, 1911).

Oregon Trunk Railroad Bridge at Crooked River, August 1911. Photographer Kelley rode his bicycle out to get this photo.

Prineville settlers could see the fires at night of the survey crews and later, the grading crews in the vicinity of Big Lake and Hogg Rock. When they suddenly pulled out, shovels, pails, picks, water jugs, and so on were left behind. For several weeks thereafter, excursions of wagons of folks from Redmond, Prineville, and Bend descended on the area, loading up whatever they could salvage that was usable.

About the same time, the California-Oregon Land Company was proposing a route to reach Bend from the south. They had many sections of land given them, but in spite of this the scheme fell through.

Again, from the east, a Mr. Stranahan, representing the Eastern Railroad to Burns, was running surveys out across the high desert.

So when the winner reached this little inland village, we had been host to several of the magnates by that time. Hill, Harriman, Stranahan, and J. D. Farrel, president of the O.W.R.N., had been in and out of this region many times. But on Railroad Day, they were all here, plus an assortment of settlers, businessmen, conmen, the curious, the booze, and the girls.

In spite of the merriment and celebrating,

certain staid and dignified ceremonies had been planned, with appropriate speeches to accompany them. So it brought down the house when someone broke through the ranks on the speaker's stand while the distinguished James J. Hill was about to begin, with, "Why, Jim Hill, you old sunnybitch! Don't you 'member me? I worked on your section gangs for the last 40 years!"

Charlie Boyd can remember overhearing a conversation between the elder Harriman, E. H., and his boy, Averell, while in the post office of this hamlet. It showed that even railroad magnates like Hill and Harriman had exchanges of down-to-earth advice for their growing boys that showed their human side.

The Harriman boy wanted some money to spend on postcards for his friends, and his dad promptly told him, "You take care of the money you get from raising chickens and you'll have some to spend!"

The old O.W.R.N. railroad was the lifeline from the Columbia River to Shaniko, bringing supplies and cutting off many miles of what would have been a rough trip on freight teams up and out of the gorge. Glen Slack was one of the newcomers riding in shortly after the turn of the century. He got visiting with a brakeman on the long, slow ride out of

Shevlin loading rig. (Slick Raper photo)

Laying log track southeast of Bend, 1929. (Munion photo)

Track laying near Bend, 1911. Publicity shot. (Francis Roberts photo)

Laying track near Bend, 1911. (Francis Roberts photo)

Shevlin track crew for the narrow gauge railroad. (Munion photo)

that mighty canyon. As they neared a particular spot on the tracks, the railroad man pointed out the window and told him that for several runs in the spring when the rattlers and other snakes were coming out of winter hibernation, they were so numerous in crossing the tracks that the engine couldn't get enough traction to made the grade on the greasy tracks.

An occasional bottle hunter or relic seeker can still see the remains of the original grade coming out of that awesome canyon.

The snakes still are residents, but are not quite that bothersome.

Oregon Trunk train arriving at Bend. (Slick Raper photo)

Pilot Butte Inn, Bend.

James J. Hill on ''Railroad Day'', Bend, October 5, 1911. (Francis Roberts)

Hotel Madras. (McCoin photo)

Hotel Shaniko. (Mrs. Thom)

CHAPTER 7

Bird Life

How long since Bend's mallards and Canada geese became tame is conjecture, but for years now they have been eating of the largess of domestic bread. Typically, from the edge of one of Bend's river parks, up past the jewelry stores and dress shops, waddles a dowager duck and a bevy of her friends.

They are on another sight-seeing spree.

It matters little that they pile up traffic six and eight cars deep across Wall Street. Unconcerned they are, too, about abiding by our speeds and our laws of progress. They slow the town to their pace of life.

Change it by running one down with your car, and you'd get off easier had you shot the mayor.

Besides the 100 or more mallards, the tolerant townspeople are intermittently blessed with honkers and swans, too. They are more aloof and harder to approach, but we are patient enough to break down their deep-bedded suspicions to eat our civilized tidbits. In the fall, the goose population burgeons with each flight from the Canadian north. Few but the bird watchers are aware of this change. The newcomers spend most of their time in the safety of the middle flowage of the Deschutes while the locals eat at the summer's end of clipped park grass. In a few days, the wilderness birds will mix with them, though, and eat their fill.

Then, in one or two frosty mornings, edging another heady day's start, some irresistible call speeds them on to Summer Lake and points south. The regulars are nervous and flighty, but know which side their bread is buttered on, and. stay.

The city swan population is eyed so closely that when there are spares of either sex, imports have been brought in to even things up in the mating department. They are always a favorite subject for camera bugs, but all the waterfowl get a good play.

Oregon is blessed with some 600 varieties of other birds, mostly because of its many life zones. The state is blessed with five zones when most states will have one or two. These read, from top to bottom, the Arctic-Alpine, the Hudsonian, the Canadian, the Transition, and the Upper Sonoran. In words of one cylinder we layman can understand, they might be called the alpine, the coniferous forest, the deciduous forest, the prairie grassland, and the desert.

To show how graphically altitude compares to miles of latitude, consider that each 1,000 feet of altitude equals 100 to 300 miles of latitude.

Oregon is a vertical land in many of its parts. It is a providential thing, too, or there would not have been room enough to put all its land within its boundaries if much of it wasn't turned on edge. This is one of the reasons that the state comes close to the richest diversity of bird life of any state in the union. From the 10,000-foot Cascade peaks where the golden eagle soars, to low desert sand pockets, home of the sedate sparrows, the dry side of the mountain range has a lifetime of bird lore to study.

Some birds are cosmopolitan. The robin is a good example. He can live under many varying conditions, as in the high fir and hemlocks at the foot of Broken Top, where he is as shy as any thrush. Robins also nest in sandy jack pine flats typical of the La Pine and Wickiup area and pare a living from those sparse surroundings. In the gardens and berry patches of central Oregon towns, they are boisterous and trusting and sassy. The robins summer in the shallow breaks of the pungent sagebrush expanses, far re-moved from their alpine cousins. Then, when dozens of lesser varieties of passerine birds have flown south, they winter in the vast juniper blanket of the desert plateau. Here the powder-blue berries, feed, melting puddles, water, and thick vegetation of certain trees protect them from zero temper-atures.

Other winter companions of these grass-lands and desert evergreens are western larks, magpies, various hawks and owls, and the crows, starlings, and sparrows.

Moving from the cosmopolitan to the specialized eventually leads us to the water ouzel. He is a highly specialized bird found in this inland area near fast, cold-running streams. Tyee Creek, Bridge or Tumalo Creeks, Fall and Spring River and the upper Deschutes flowages are his stamping grounds. The water ouzel is a small, thrush-like bird that feeds on insects in creek and stream bottoms. He will fly low over the water surface and suddenly dive under, breasting the current, walking and feeding for many feet. Often, his nest is behind the protecting flow of a waterfall in the rocks. Here he must fly through the cascading water to reach the sheltered but dry nesting spot. The water ouzel's feathers are oiled quite often from glands that he uses in preening himself in order to waterproof feathers again. His tail, held high like a wren's, dips up and down constantly while he moves about; hence, in many places, he is called the teeter or dipper.

The yellow-headed and red-winged black-birds are commonplace and merely start the list. Flickers, finches, grosbeaks, warblers,

woodpeckers, orioles, hummingbirds, mag-pies, crows, jays, and bluebirds abound as dry-siders of the Cascades. Sparrows, hawks, and owls come in infinite variety.

Some late week in August or early Sep-tember brings one bird peculiar to the Bend-Redmond area. The arrival of the juniper jays is perhaps the first notable announcement from the avian world that fall is near. In flocks of 30 to 40, they feed — loudly — through the ponderosa treetops, occasionally dropping to someone's lawn, turning it a living blue in a flash. Their harsh, metallic cries bring vague premonitions about wood-piles and coal bills to the dour townspeople on the far side of 60. To the young in heart, to the hunter, to the skier, it is celestial oratory of happy times to come.

One other bird is worthy of a separate write-up. He doesn't comport himself with much grace on the ground or in flight, but the magpie is wary as the crow. He is no easy target for a youngster with his first .22. They keep our highways clean of dead rabbits and chipmunks. The ungainly flight and the parson dress of this long-tailed bird is typically a western scene. They tough out most of our winters, too.

The Paulina Mountains are a travel route for many bird strangers during the October deer season on the flight south. Here are

Avian Spectacle

Hands down, the star of the songsters for color is the western tanager. Anyone who has ever been graced with a sighting of him will never forget him. The late irrigation ditches have brought numerous newcomers. We say "late" — they have been here for thousands of years, and the birds have been around for millions of years. The birds can get along without us, but we can't get along without them, neither very profitably nor happily.

seen ground feeders, creepers, and treetop flitters, all passing through those timbered hills in company of each other. Then the snaking wedges of cacklers and geese float overhead to forecast a storm for the nimrods that didn't bring a radio for a weather report. This is sufficient warning of foul weather coming to a weather-wise hunter.

The bird gunners have a good choice of upland game. Four or five kinds of quail, sage hens, chukars, ring-necked pheasant, doves, and woodcock fill the menu for the most discriminating scatter-gunner. Turkeys were lately planted in parts of this plateau country, near the ghost town of Grandview, and a season was held on them. A gunner must know his calls, his stalking, his choice of rifle and bullet, or shotgun and shot to bag this wary bird.

But another game bird about the same size and weight is much less cautious. The sage hen, so called by the homesteaders, or sage grouse, was a feathered blessing when meat was scarce on the desert. He was brought low with rocks, bullwhips, .22's, and shotguns — these in the hands of greenhorn hunters. The meat, if taken care of, is of the finest. Today, a short season still leads the leg-weary bird shooters far and wide, circling the desert in quest of the sometimes foolish, sometimes sly sage grouse.

Wherever a cluster of aspens or a lone poplar have thrust down roots in the desert places, one can be sure there is water in that draw. Anyone familiar with the desert knows these trees are out of place unless there is a spring or a hidden source of water. The simple fact of these trees means a new species of bird — or two or three — nesting in this oasis surrounded by scrub desert. How long it takes them to find these places is unknown, but it is no doubt on a trip south some fall when they tuck the spot away in their brain. Spring may find them flying

unerringly to it, to scrap for a piece of that territory with other males.

It could well be a red-winged blackbird in a place like this. He is as much at home here as in a marsh in northern Canada or beside any western irrigation ditch.

Grown men still remember a night camp-out as frightened boys, wildly guessing what creature screamed or who-whoed off in the night. The owl could always do more damage to already jumpy nerves. These heavily feathered raptors spend their winters here, also.

While winter sees most songsters head south, tail feathers and all, the hardy sparrow, the magpies, the chipper juncos and chickadees, grosbeaks, the scrounging woodpeckers and flickers, and latercomer finches and starlings tough out normal mid-state winters.

Four o'clock in the afternoon will find low-skimming hawks on aerial prowls for a mouse. Sparrow hawks are country phone wire fixtures, where they warm in the last rays of winter sun.

A prime way to beat the monotony of winter days is to sweep a six-or eight-foot area clean to the grits and dirts near shrubs and trees. Here, regular feeding of scratch feed and suet will repay the donor with the small satisfaction that he has pulled some of our bird life through a tough winter, when they may not have made it. An added dividend is in learning a small page in the endless volumes open to those who are curious about the wildlings.

Then, in mid-March, when the blithe spirit of spring returns with a dagger in her hand, the first song sparrow will sound its flute along riverbank. Other wild scarves of color, flying in on the tattered ends of winter, will stoutly defend a little territory, sounding off to a winter-weary world that the sun is returning to central Oregon.

CHAPTER 8

Just Kids

"In 1907, my nephew and I took our bikes and rode the 75 miles from Prineville to Shaniko, on terrible roads, to catch the Columbia Southern Railroad to Portland to see a circus we heard about."

This was Doc Ketchum reminiscing about his childhood. His dad, an early comer to Prineville, made boots to order in the 1890's.

That was the day of bike travel by highwheelers, too. But the boys only remember one man in Prineville who had one. He was a banker by the name of Mr. Baldwin.

That must have rated him as a person of some affluence, about like having the first color TV set. You were in.

In those days they couldn't tell bothersome kids to go play on the freeway. It was probably "Go sort wildcats" if they lived in the country; or "Go play with the fuse box" when the first electricity hit the inland towns.

Maybe they didn't speak until spoken to, but kids will be kids, and were in those days, too.

Mrs. Joe Conninger remembers the Halloween night the boys made the rounds and harnessed all the cows in town with horse harnesses. Every kid knew how to make a noisemaker that rattled on a window pane at night like a ghost's knuckles. Kids had no "made" recreation. If they could get a vacant lot or pasture, a ball game was started. A pick or peavey handle was much used as a substitute for a bat in the absence of the real McCoy. And any boy worth his salt could, and did, sew the covers on the balls as they started tearing loose. This was done over and over again until they were so mushy they couldn't be hit past second base.

Shingles were treasured for making short arrows to shoot with a piece of inner tube and string on a handle. The right combination of ingredients could put one of these out of sight in the sky.

Another homemade toy was the propeller shooter. A propeller was cut out of a tin so the finished blade was four or five inches long. An empty spool had two brads nailed into one end about half an inch apart. Holes to fit over these were punched into the tin propeller. The spool, wound with string, was dropped down over a sucker stick. When the string was pulled hard, the propeller spun up and off the stick high into the air in a blur of motion. It floated gracefully from 60 to 80 feet up.

A golf ball was a real find. The cover was carefully cut off so yards and yards of thin rubber binding could unwind between two running boys who listened with glee to the ghostly whir as the wind rippled the rubber. Of course, the soft, mushy core of the ball was "filled with poison."

Stripling cowboys made their own chaps out of an old rug with diagonally slashed leather strips sewed to them for show. An old pop bottle cap had the cork inner liner carefully removed, and shoved back into place from inside a shirt — this was the sheriff's badge. Those that didn't whittle their six-guns used a stray piece of one-by-four for their rubber gun; these flipped tight-pulled inner tube binders to kill flies against the barn or on the porch ceiling.

Ken Maynard, Hoot Gibson, Tom Mix, and Buck Jones were the heroes of the day.

City kids had their "hoop and wheel" for pushing most of their waking hours. Just a lath with a crosspiece nailed on the bottom and a spare wagon or baby buggy wheel put them in business. A boy proficient in this art could carry a sack of groceries in one hand and never have a spill with his wheel all the way home.

A gang of kids that had a homemade crystal set were millionaires. The crystal, a cantankerous little piece of metal, had only two or three places the needle or feeler could get some far-off program. One or two kids shared earphones while the third pushed the slide bar across the copper wire wound around the oatmeal box or cylinder until the right wavelength was found.

All kites were made of newspaper and sticks and struts split with a pocketknife. Tails were swiped off mothers who saved rag strips for rugs or quilts. Masters of kite-making graduated to box kites, with pull enough to give a small kid a tussle in holding them. It took a competent junior engineer to put one of these together. Once in the air, it was the thing to do to tie them to a tree or ride out the night winds until morning. Then navigators and pilots choked down a fast breakfast to take the helm again.

Games faintly remembered, but never mentioned now, were Run Sheep Run; Green Light, Red Light; Prisoner's Base; Canny-Can; Stillwater; Pump Pump Pullaway; mumblety-peg; jacks; baseball (with a knife); and many others. These kept kids engrossed for hours on end before that initiative-killer, TV, came along.

To take the monotony away from lessons in school, each boy had a tractor made of a large empty thread spool. A rubber binder was pushed in the spool hole and twisted tight, with a short match on one end and a full length on the other. The end with the long match was waxed or soaped so it would slip. Notches cut in the spool's rim enabled them to climb a book "being studied."

One girl skipping along through those halcyon days remembers a particularly glorious night when fire swept several buildings in Bend, mostly saloons. There were bottles "popping all over the place," she said. But the men stood around shaking their heads, saying it was a terrible waste.

In one section of the county, a big, strawberry roan horse named Kit was a forerunner of the school bus service. A Sisters resident told of how she and four other kids rode that horse to and from school for several years, all astride her ample back.

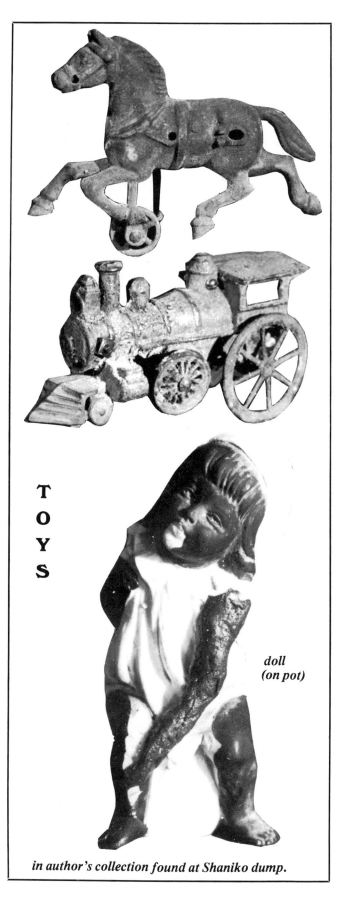

**T
O
Y
S**

*doll
(on pot)*

in author's collection found at Shaniko dump.

Outhouse Humor

The seats of the outhouses and inhouses at the old Reid school of Bend were painted with a thick, green paint by the boys one memorable night. Some of the girls knew, but were threatened if they snitched. It was not the usual paint. A peculiarity it had was that it would not dry, even after many days. It had to be scrubbed off. What treatments the unfortunate-seated victims used, no one volunteered.

Others talked of their home life. They mentioned pine needle pillows, straw ticks, sheepskin pads, and feather tick covers. Winters got cold in this inland plateau. Mrs. Brick Laird and Jess Tetherow told of nails popping like rifle shots during cold snaps. Another housewife, green and innocent in this new life, imagined it was the Indians coming by at night, throwing rocks at the windows, and was terrified at the sound.

Orissa Sears told of the annual ritual of taking up homemade rugs and removing the year-old straw underneath; floors were scrubbed with lye water before spreading a new three-inch layer of straw for warmth.

All hands were needed to pull the rugs back again, tight, tight, and tacked around the edges for another winter. These floors were warm enough for creeping babies and kids laying on their bellies eating popcorn.

Kids all had their chores, however simple, around the relatively primitive homes. While this was drudgery for some, for others it wasn't. The Boyd girls shared the small task of bringing eggs in each day with their brother. They got their heads together and decided they weren't earning enough. "When we'd get short of change, we would put eggs under the hens again, and collect twice," they said. "Our folks should have walloped us for that."

They also fondly recalled a "half-baked" team their dad had that was always running away with them. "Us kids would go just sailing out of that wagon!"

Mrs. Weigand, then of Lamonta, used to put the tiny ones on blankets out in the fields while she and the older children pulled and grubbed the eternal sagebrush.

As seen from many an old snapshot, the kids went to school barefoot. This didn't detract from the lessons being taught. Most early teachers were volunteers, hired at a monthly salary. Most recalled the pay as being $35 a month at most schools, teaching lasting for three to four months.

When the inland towns got cultural enough to have a high school, most children had to leave home. They would board and room with strangers and were gone from their families for weeks at a time. For shy country kids, this was a sad experience. The only high spots remembered were the Easter and Christmas vacations and the rides home in sleighs heated with rocks, kids snuggled underneath horsehair robes or blankets. Talk was a mile a minute in getting caught up on all the happenings.

The schools had another function. Debate teams and literary societies were active in

every village and hamlet. The thirst for knowledge or politics or expressing themselves could not be stilled.

"We gave readings and plays, and debated hot issues of the times," one man told me. Attendance was good and everybody joined in. The rustic life seemed to be counterbalanced with this sort of thing.

A groundwork in numbers, citizenship, and grammar sufficed for many who took the reins of responsibility early in life.

"We were not too proud to pledge allegiance to our flag," some said. Some teachers opened their class with a morning prayer.

The boys grew tall to the sun, as men should, and mothers raised families cushioned with love but bordered with a stern discipline when needed.

The birth of athletics between Bend and Prineville was told in intimate details by Claude Kelley, who played football on that first team from here in 1912: "We were not supposed to practice school nights or play a game with another school or we would be expelled, our superintendent told us. But all the arrangements had been made to ride to Prineville for a game. We went in a long-bedded wagon with side curtains on it to keep out the wind. Ralph Lucas drove us over. We had a treat at Niswonger's stage stop in Powell Butte.

"We all had places to stay at private homes, and the townspeople had a big basket social and dance planned at their school gym. That night it snowed four or five inches. We were beaten pretty badly as they had a well-coached team, and we had been practicing surreptitiously.

"We didn't get expelled, and more games followed. At that time, it was a day over, a day there, and a day back by team, for that 35-mile trip."

From small beginnings, the intermountain league has grown to boast some of the strongest teams in the state.

But no more pop stops at Niswonger's stage stop.

The galvanized washtub in front of the kitchen range held as many protesting kids in those days as we hear in a plush bathroom today. And how many young ones remember having to wash in the second water of the wash basin behind an elder when water was scarce?

A woodbox waited to be filled while a young one watched, caught up in the eternity of an instant, as a blue wasp caught a cutworm, stung it to death, dug a pit to bury it in, and laid its egg with it — the source of its baby's food a completed task.

Weeding a garden took second place over a pair of coyote pups watching, with cocked head and curious eyes, the first human they had ever seen.

The noise of wood splitting in the fall quieted suddenly at the call of wild geese pulsating past in a sky muttering up a storm.

"Do they get tired?"

"How far have they come?"

"Which one knows the way?"

These and many other questions fluttered into a young mind in a moment indelible with wonder and beauty, transcending time itself. At this pause, their pulse was one with God's universe.

It mattered little in classroom if a boy knew a deer track from an antelope's, or a bobcat's from a dog's, but it was an art that few could decipher, and therefore it was a fine achievement.

Children incline their ear more to Nature and notice much that older folks are blind to.

Their first watch, one of a thousand sparkling nights in cattle land, on their own horse, with winter mornings like tempered silver, when fragments of beauty dropped from bunchgrass in a moping sun — all this they knew. They were closer than earth to Nature, feeling, touching, knowing its moods in a fresh innocence we haven't known since a child either.

It's a shame this finer part of being a child couldn't stay with some of us as adults.

One morning, winter bestirs itself by rattling its sabers — dead limbs against window panes — and the kids complain how cold the sheets are in that unheated bedroom, so they pad along behind as mom gets out the flannel ones. These are much cozier to climb into, they remember. Then the cedar chest or trunk is opened, letting the smell of mothballs seep through the house. And the longjohns are spread out in piles, sorted to size.

Winter is officially here.

First school in Bend was in what is now Drake Park. Photographer, Claude Kelley rode his bicycle to take hundreds of photos.

Mrs. Slack, center back, was a schoolteacher for many years. She and husband Glen home-steaded five miles south of Bend. This is the early 1900's. (Glen Slack photo)

Lonnie Weaver's grandad donated an acre of land for the Montgomery School, eleven miles down river from Prineville. Note the barefoot children. Lottie Montgomery, Charles McDowell, Bernard Tetherow, Jess Tetherow, Burns Montgomery, Mark Forest, Barnard Forest, Cellia Forest, Aylette Tetherow, John McDowell, Mary McDowell, Ann McDowell, Charlie Weaver, Lonnie Weaver, Earl Forest, Jane Messinger, Lula Montgomery, Edna Bethel. Teacher: Lina Dillion.

CHAPTER 9

Lumbering

The "pondosa" pines, as most early-day references to them were, probably did more to develop central Oregon than any other single thing, except the people themselves.

It is peculiar that this spelling is encountered only in the older periodicals and papers. Now they are the ponderosa, yellow or western yellow. The trees have a beautiful red-brown bark that always looks as if they had been scrubbed ruddy and clean. The young trees are blacker-looking and are dubbed blackjack or bull pine by the woodsmen. They are remarkable trees insofar as they can grow on land almost as arid as the juniper does.

An estimated 16 billion board feet of this timber lay in a huge semicircle south of Bend in 1915. These figures were stated in a Chamber of Commerce paper covering the advent of the ambitious mills just moving into Bend. The two mills, Shevlin-Hixon and Brooks-Scanlon, for years had an annual capacity of almost 400 million board feet and a yearly payroll of about $4,000,000. It is little wonder that this potential served as the vitamin pills Bend needed to grow to manhood.

One resident put it this way: "Bend was a good town when Shevlin was here — everybody had money." But when Shevlin sold its interests to Brooks, about Christmas of 1950, it took the town several years to shake off that blow. Many families had to move away.

One of the mills in its heyday had a total of 1,500 to 1,800 men in the yards, mill, and woods. Fifteen to twenty-two cars of lumber were loaded and sent out each day to waiting markets.

For better than 35 years, the logs were hauled in by log train from many parts of the compass. Southeast, south, southwest, and west lay the heavy cuts, but northwest towards Sisters the stands thinned to hemlock and fir. The juniper forests lay in a small arc north of Bend and Redmond. While several attempts were made for their use in making pencils, the junipers are still relatively unused commercially.

The trains made a goodly haul of 125 cars of logs a day, two runs per day. On the trip to Bend, mostly downgrade, one engine was used on the main lines. But on the return run out again, even the empties needed a double-header as far as Lava Butte.

The track crews lay track a year ahead of the cutters. This almost forgotten phase of the logging days had several interesting features. Tie mills were set up in many places in the countryside by enterprising operators. Among them mentioned were Archie Pepin, Jim Whitlock, Nick Meyers, and Roy Larson.

The railroad ties were jack pine, slabbed on two sides. When the day of the colorful log train came to an end, many tons of used rails were shipped abroad to Japan. The demise of the trains came in the fifties.

Each large camp had its storeroom that sold to families living in camp. Erickson's Market of Bend brought groceries by truck once a week or so on a loose schedule for any that wanted fresh produce. The huge quantities of grub for hungry log crews came in carload lots by train once a week. It was big business when as many as 135 families, for example, lived in the Chemult camp.

Of course, men bragged of their exploits then as now, so one month, to spice things up, a cutting contest was held. Two-man crosscut saws were used, with the men cutting six days a week. The winners were Paul Peterson and Jack Galvon, downing

608,000. Billy Frenzel and his partner, Harold Grass, were second, with the Talbot brothers a close third, at 550,000.

Any itinerant timber beast looking for work got set up with a partner. Between them, they got a 6½-foot saw, with a newly sharpened substitute each morning, two axes, and a dozen wedges furnished. They each carried their own oil bottle (though it was more kerosene than oil) slung in a pouch on their hip to combat pitch. With the ever-prevalent fire danger, when an oil bottle was forgotten or lost, another was not issued until the stray and its remnants were found. All glass bottles and jars at the campsites were diligently buried to prevent the sun's rays from focusing through them and causing a fire.

These camps, of course, moved from cutting to cutting. Shevlin was the woods town name for years, by special arrangement with the United States Post Office. That little chore took some doing because the brass in Washington, D.C., had never run into this sort of thing before. But the deal was swung, and the transient town had the unique distinction of being the most moved post office in the U.S. They had a store, cook shack, blacksmith shop, office and timekeeper shacks, and a building furnished for a school. Many of the young citizens of Shevlin camps were born when it was a tent camp. Near-zero weather ushered some of them into this

Lumberjacks in tall timber. (Earl Talbot photo)

world. When school-agers needed tutoring, they weren't sent to town, unless the parents elected to do so. Three of those camp teachers were Maude Catlow, Mary Schuler, and Evelyn Caldwell.

Horses were the power in those legendary days and, at one time, the mill used as many as 250 a day for various chores. Some they owned, most they rented, for about $1 per day. Clint Olson kept records of the horses, as with the men, giving description, color, weight, age, and so on for each animal rented or owned. Then at end of the month, he made two checks for each horse, one for the company and another for Aune's livery barn.

Mrs. Stella Nelson told of "Old Dock," the horse that sat. He was a huge animal and evidently did this to take the weight off his feet. The lumber camp kids used to love to go up to him and feed him goodies every day he was in camp. There the big lug sat, all 2,000 pounds of him, like a dog, mooching goodies off his junior jack friends.

Others of his kind sat and skidded on those huge rumps when they had heavy loads to hold on a downhill drag.

The ponderosa pine is the number one tree in Oregon, moneywise. Another, the sugar pine, is probably more beautiful, more poetic in aspect, and has more colorful wood. But it can be put into the dry kilns in boards and came out slats. This bad habit of checking is not nearly so prevalent in this tree grown in

How Much Was It Worth?

From the twenties to the forties, wages varied from 71¢ per thousand cut a day, to 91¢, for the timber bucks. Back at camp, a company camp, bachelors paid $3 a day for eats, and they were good. The cabin came to $3 a month for rent, lights, and water, with wood furnished.

School-age kids in the camp could make a dime or 20¢ at each shack by the splitting of several blocks of body wood, dead blue-skinned stuff. It was quick money, and a dime could buy something then. A cluster of shacks lined up for splitting heater chunks kept an enterprising lad in good pocket money.

California. Some standing trees are wind-checked; upon being felled, they will lay in splinters, completely unusable. John Muir, the great naturalist, called this tree "the largest, noblest and most beautiful of all the 70 or 80 pines." It has the largest cones of any pine in the world; some of them measure 16" to 18" in length.

Few regions in the world have greater reserves of timber than Oregon. Spruce, hemlock, Douglas fir, white fir, cedar, larch, and white pine carpet the high ranges of the state. Recently, the lodgepole or jack pine stands are being harvested, and the wood is being cut and used in furniture manufacture.

The age of these various trees is always an interesting topic. Patriarchs cut down in Bend in past years have been standing around looking the country over for five centuries or more. Yet the oldest living things in the state are the juniper men. Some of these will possibly be twice that age, and more.

In taking a walk through the woods, one can see remnants of huge yellow pine felled years ago with the top third or quarter unused and unlimbed. That day is gone. While this was a commonplace thing when the cuts seemed endless, now every part of a tree is used. And since competition with the plastics will get keener, still more prefab wood products are sure to follow.

Take the aforementioned walk in the timbered areas with an old lumberjack and he can tell much by merely looking at a stump: if it was a summer or winter cut, if it leaned, how it leaned, whether the pitch was unusually high in the stump, and many other things a novice would miss.

Some of the woodsmen were river-runners, as an old hand put it, "so good you couldn't shoot them off a log with a shotgun." The last big log drive of about 30 million board feet was down the sometimes wild, sometimes placid and deep Deschutes. The run was from Pringle Falls to Benham Falls. Jim Cook was on that one, and there were stories to tell.

Among those spun was the one about four lumberjacks returning from a dance at La Pine to the Summit Stage Camp early on a Sunday morning. As usual at these affairs, whether a homesteader hoedown or a timber tango, there were spirits in some form or other. Bootleg, homemade, or entirely legal, it all had the same, happy end effect, as these participants found out that memorable night.

One of them had a Plymouth. Two rode in the front seat and the third had the back to himself. There was much banter and hell-raising at the dance, so they had plenty to gas about on the trip back to camp.

Suddenly the front riders realized their backseat buddy was pretty quiet. When they turned around to have him verify something, they were aghast! He was gone!

The roads those days were rough with a capital "R," so when the little Plymouth hit a long, smooth stretch, the luckless victim in back thought the car had stopped and he opened the door and stepped out — at 40 miles an hour.

All hell broke loose, and the two men careened back and forth getting turned around to find their buddy, expecting the worst. Three or four miles back they found a shoe in the road, and then the lights picked up the figure of their pal sitting smack in the middle of the straightaway, rubbing his head.

"We thought he'd be dead," one volunteered, "but outside of some bruises and abrasions, he was all right.

"We took him to camp and made some coffee, the accepted treatment for lumberjack flu, and sat up till morning. I don't know why, but we didn't do much to clean him up. You could take one look at his eyes and tell what type blood he had. We went back to La Pine that morning to buy breakfast. The waitress took one look at him and gasped, "What happened to him?"

"We knew she would never believe us, so we said he just got back from Tokyo."

"Where there is wood, there can be fire. Several of the early settlers spun tales of their memories of the "big woods" burning. And any discerning hunter will note he can walk in few sections of our forests that are free of charred wood.

The old stage road from Bend to Prineville has large sections of the great junipers destroyed by fire. No doubt, these were caused

Logs for Masten Lumber Company, 1910. (Slick Raper photo)

by pipes or cigars that were smoked by some careless skinners or the occupants of their wagon.

Claude Vandevert and others rocked back in their chairs while recounting the Edison Ice Cave conflagration or some other one, little remembered. Claude's brother and a Mr. Edison discovered the ice cave while mopping up on that blaze in 1910.

The Paulina Mountains had many acres burned out two years earlier than the Edison fire. Hunters prowling this remote ridge can still see charred wood scattered all through that spine of land.

By piecing together their memories, and gathering notes from U.S. Forest Service annals, the following major conflagrations have been recorded:

The Paulina Mountains fire took place in 1908. "Several sections," said an oldster.

In 1910 was the Edison Ice Cave fire, some 20 miles southwest of Bend, about 8,000 acres in size.

1926 was the year of the Fox Butte blaze, according to Forest Service officials; it blackened about 10,000 acres of ponderosa. That same year, the Fremont had an extensive section burned out. 1926 seemed to be a bad fire year because Sisters residents told of the Green Ridge burning above the Metolius that same summer.

1930 saw the Dugout Lake fire, according to the official records. Closer to home, the Big Springs-Kiwa Springs area had its inferno that first year of the thirties.

1938 was the year of the Indian reservation blaze of over 100,000 acres, on the Warm Springs lands.

Seemingly unrecorded are fire-burned sections on both sides of the road west to Wickiup Dam.

The 1959 burn was the largest of the last trio of woods holocausts, involving Aspen Flat, Big Lake, and Coyote Butte. The first-mentioned fire blackened yellow pine flats from Pilot Butte in the north to the Devils Garden sector to the south.

Hoodoo Bowl's slopes and part of their facilities fell to uncontrolled blazes in the Big Lake burning in the middle sixties.

The Coyote Butte fire and scores of small spot fires punctuate the forest green with grim reminders of what might have been.

These are our woods. It is well to remember that each of us had a stake in their welfare by commonsense use of matches, smokes, and camps.

As indicated earlier, this was — and is — juniper land. A green sea of the old men of the desert rolls in gentle waves from the edge of the Deschutes to the breaks of the Owyhee. These disheveled patriarchs grow in a pitiless arid region of five to fifteen inches annual rainfall.

Junipers have some attributes.

They are a tough, aromatic member of the cedar family. Their posts held countless miles of barbed wire. Their fallen needles were a primitive insulation when held in a double-wall construction; there are still a few buildings in central Oregon that have walls filled with this dry material.

The gnarled, twisted limbs were a poor bet for lumber, as were the trunks. The mature trees invariably have hollowed trunks and limbs. Yet, from a tale told here and the remnants of a fallen building there, we have a faintly persistent rumor of the so-called "Juniperus squarus."

"I remember Uncle Bill telling of seeing a pile of square limbs on so-and-so's place," one man said. Or again, "A buckaroo told of a line cabin southeast of Frederick Butte with vertical walls made of square juniper." And so it went.

A former cook for one of Bill Brown's camps told a long, legendary tale that ran something like this:

"I was on the trail of a couple of stray cows one cold spring morning. The wind cut like a hunter's knife as I tracked them east of Whittaker Holes.

"I passed a cave, one of them flat-holed openings in the desert floor you could ride by within 15 feet and miss it. But I kept on and in a mile or so saw smoke rising blue over a little outcrop.

"There was a shack with a woodshed and barn attached to one side and a chicken pen and outhouse further off. They must have just started the fire because smoke rings were puffing out of the chimney like them big ones the one-lung threshing machines used to make.

"It was cold and the rings sailed up lazy-like and drifted off. But there was something mighty peculiar about them, and you won't believe this.

"Them rings of smoke were square!

"Now I've seen hundreds of chimneys in my time, all square, but they didn't make no square rings of smoke.

"This'n did.

"Anyways, a guy stuck his head out the

Deep snow in '49 at Shevlin Camp. (Munion photo)

door and invited me in, which I did because I was slowly congealing from the godawful cold. The everpresent coffee pot and tea kettle were settin' on top of the stove, just startin' to sing. I could smell sourdoughs, which his woman presently took out of the oven.

"In talkin' to them, they hadn't seen my critters, but that was possibly because they had turned south behind the rise and went on.

"After eating, I thawed by the stove for a spell exchanging small gossip before mounting to ride on again. As I walked by the woodshed, there was a sawhorse and some chunks of square-barked juniper limbs for the stove. I turned to ask them where they had got the wood, but the door was shut. And I plumb forgot to mention them damn smoke-rings when I smelled the biscuits.

"I caught up with my critters circling back, then cut straight home to the northwest.

"Later, I got work with Bill Brown when things got tough and worked out of the camp near Wagontire Mountain. I mentioned the square wood a couple times, but the hands laughed at me, so I knew better than telling about the rings I had seen.

"But one morning a new hand come ridin'

in. I was cookin' then and I got to hit it off pretty well with him while I fixed him some grub. The others were out riding for broomtails. The new guy had brought a quart of good bootleg with him, so before the others came driftin' in, we proceeded to lower the contents of that bottle.

"After talkin' horses and huntin' for a spell, he said to me if I wouldn't laugh, he'd tell me something. I promised not to laugh.

"Then he told me of seein' a whole parcel of them square-limbed junipers while ridin' up from Silver Lake. He said someone had been cuttin' hell out of them, but there were still some left. Then I told him about the smokerings, and he believed me.

"I was stuck in camp for a long time, but I made a good grubstake, so I stayed on. When

I had enough to pick up some land near Bend, I got paid off.

"On the way in, I was positive I'd find that settlers's shack and get me a chunk of that square juniper, but I swung too far north, I guess.

"But I know I saw what I saw and I heard what I heard, so take it or leave it."

And that's how the story was told to me. Now, I'm not a scientist, but a kind of historian writing what I heard. Maybe, just maybe there lies out there in that vast graygreen sea of sage a scattering of *Juniperus squarus* hidden in a small wash or basin. Or have they vanished like the legendary, but very real, lava bear did?

Only the desert gods know.

CHAPTER 10

Gold!

Gold has held a fascination for all nations and their peoples. This is equally true for Oregon and its geographical parts.

Many old-timers had gold stories to tell concerning localities they traversed. It might come as a surprise, then, to hear of some of them coming out of the heart of a land resting wave upon wave and layer on layer of lava, such as central Oregon rests on.

In 1907, Charles Carrol, Jess Harter, Bill Hunt, and four others, unidentified, got together a pack string and headed for old Broken Top Mountain on a gold-hunting expedition. They stayed for days, panning creeks, moraine lakes, and drywashes, seeking the yellow metal, but the only traces they found were at the east foot of South Sister. So they reluctantly went back to more prosaic means of making their living.

Mrs. Jess Harter supplied the narration of this, one of the first references to gold-seekers at the turn of the century.

Another of the notable finds was told by the Glen Slack family, who had a homestead five miles south of Pilot Butte at that time. They had a neighbor, Mr. Billadieau, who was digging and lining a cistern. Any prospector worth a small nugget knows that lava country makes for poor gold pickin' — but is it true? As the man was working on his project, a section of it fell away and he was amazed to see the dull glitter of gold in a crevice there. The Slacks did not recall what their neighbor received from his find. Then, some time later, Mrs. Slack bought some chickens for killing from a neighbor in another direction from them. Upon cleaning their crops, she found two nuggets in them.

One they sold for $2.50 and the other for $7.50.

Surprisingly, no prospecting followed those finds. But other locations having gold rushes — or finds — include Cline Buttes, Broken Top, Brown's Mountain, North Sister, and an area roughly between Diamond Lake and Elk Lake. Of course, several came out of the tight-hilled Ochocos where, it seems, every little creek has its trace of gold.

Ed Harris was on his way to Idaho to work in the mines, but he needed meat. Near Sand Springs, southeast of Bend, he shot an antelope. The wounded animal led him to a shallow draw filled with black sand that seemed much out of place in the usual pumice sand of the desert. Ed filled one of his saddle bags, as he was curious about his unusual find. He headed for Whitaker Holes north of Pine Mountain and eventually, when he found water enough, panned it out. The sand proved rich. Ed thought he marked the spot well in his mind, but upon coming back several years later with relatives, not once but several times, could find nothing that dovetailed with his memory.

In early-day Prineville, reference was made to another find: "C. P. Johnson is in partnership with Mr. Cannon, and they are operating two hydraulics on the property . . . and on one occasion they found a nugget that sold for four hundred and sixty-eight dollars." [1]

The Frenchmen's Mine, somewhere between Diamond Lake and Elk Lake, yielded wealth the first year of operation. The owners captured an Indian woman on their return trip but were tracked to their cabin and killed

---

[1] *An Illustrated History of Central Oregon*, p. 671.

Mr. Harter of Sisters. He organized a gold expedition in 1909 up around Broken Top.

by five members of that tribe. One of the Indians returned several times, carrying out gold, but no one ever succeeded in tracking him to its source.

As a young man, W.O. Wood remembered meeting some Callapooya Indians coming back to the valley after their annual trek in the North Sister area. They did this in the fall when there was a low snowpack for their winter supply money. This particular day, they were broken down with a splintered wagon wheel west of the Cascades. The Woods party got some haywire and other gear, helped with the repairs, and got them on their way. The grateful Indians told them this much: They came from a section north or northwest of the mountain, high up. But that venerable mountain has countless wrinkles on its face in the form of dry washes, low ridges, creek flows, and rock flows sufficient enough to hide the Indians' secret to all but a persistent prospector.

Another yarn from Prineville went as follows: "It was in 1907 or '08 as near as I can recall," the narrator said, trying to jog his memory, "when a man came riding from east of town with samples in his bags. We could tell from his horse that he had been riding

hard and long. But it turned out the rider got the worst of that trip. He picked up a sore from the long ride that quickly got an infection in it. He died from blood poisoning. The stuff was rich, but he never talked, so we didn't learn the source of it."

In drilling a well on the King Ranch, Mr. Sakry of Bend told of mucky black sand being brought up with traces of gold all through it, in the core.

The upper Deschutes flowage had a handful of settlers before and during the time the logging people started moving across the land. One of these was a Negro fellow known by all his friends and neighbors as Nigger Brown. Brown's Mountain and Brown's Creek still bear his name. Grover Caldwell told of the man's mining operations in the summer and his trapping during the winter; he was a good trapper and a fine woodsman. His wife was Mexican, and the pair had several children. During the summer, he saved his meager supply of gold, and in the fall he headed on the long trek across the timberlands to Prineville to supply his family and himself for the long winter of trapping. Spring snows melted in puddles as he bundled his furs for the jaunt back for the fur

Nuggets, Nuggets Everywhere

The Van Lake brothers, homesteading the west slopes of Hampton Butte, took leave of ranching one time for a trip over the slopes to the northeast. They saddled up, filled a water jug, pocketed some sandwiches, and took off to look for what the desert had to offer. They at last came to an extensive, sandy, wind-blown area with dead junipers in it. They dismounted and Van went over to a particularly large tree. According to Van, his brother said, "This looks like a good place to look for gold." So they were scooping and probing in the sand when Van felt something hard in a handful. When the sand was blown off it, it was found to be the size of a dried pea, wrinkled, and gold. His brother later sold out and moved to Arizona, had the nugget mounted in a tiepin and wore it for years.

Center, a descendant of an old prospector. 1916.
(Brookings photo)

buyer to assess his catch for another grub-stake. Few remember that pioneer today and none ever learned where his diggings were. Somewhere under acres of snowbrush and manzanita in some little creek bed, they may be resumed.

It was inevitable that several should mention the now-legendary Blue Bucket train. Two of them had relatives in that ill-fated party. As they neared the mighty Columbia, they stopped to make rafts. A baby was put in one of the huge cast-iron, three-legged cooking kettles, with a pad of several blankets. Near midstream, the load shifted, tilting the raft. A young mother screamed and ran for the skidding kettle, but it slid off into the murky waters to drown her little one.

There were oxen in that immigrant train, and this fact governed how many miles they could travel each day, probably no more than eight or ten. All known evidence seems to indicate that they were four days from Pilot Butte at the time of the gold find. That would put them 40 miles east of here, and possibly only 32. This is in the Bear Creek country.

One of the men interviewed spent much time in that area because his folks had a homestead there. The young man spent long hours and days riding and exploring it. He said that in the ensuing years there have been many drastic changes there. Dry washes, once strewn with rocks, agate, and mineral are now drifted full of blown sand or washed full from waterspouts and thunderstorms that have added inches to their bottoms each year. But this same man is convinced that the searchers are wasting their time in looking for gold any farther than 30 or 40 miles east of Bend. This vicinity is mostly out of the lava flow.

We also have traces and reports and actual diggings of coal, tin, uranium, cinnabar, and talc products such as oromite in this inland country.

Bear Creek, north of Ashwood, has its share of mercury mines. A scramble in all directions for metal detectors and geiger counters came with the advent of the government's interest in precious earths some years back. Only one plant blossomed from all the searching, that in the Lakeview sector.

Oil drill rigs moved inconspicuously all over the face of our desert for another decade or two. If the probings held any promise, the facts, ma'am, have been kept mighty quiet. This writer has found many capped casings on his numerous desert excursions in the past many years. Not all are abandoned water wells.

John Silvertooth, of Antelope, and Lonnie Weaver, of Bend, roamed the sage and juniper lands many times on probes of their own. They found tin deposits. The samples were sent to a mining firm in England for assaying, but nothing came of it, Lonnie said.

Poor grades of coal have been discovered and samples picked by rockhounds. Others have brought back oil-soaked sand from the Crooked River scablands. One gentleman showed me his cigar box full of it that burned with a somewhat blue flame. The box, tucked away in a corner of his basement, was layered in dust since put away there in the late thirties.

Oregon diamonds, so-called, have been found on the flanks of Wagontire Mountain. Another friend of mine had beautifully faceted gems that Tiffany's in New York polished and mounted for him. These were in delicate shades of amber, blue, green, and pink.

Another persistent tale is of a copper find

in a canyon near Mount Jefferson. Allegedly, some hikers discovered it when losing the trail. It was "so pure it could not be blasted, but only gouged out." This is in a wilderness area, so it is off limit for mining interest.

Like the tin discovery, this is a story that could well be worth someone's time to run down. Then again, it might be yet another tale that grows and enriches with each telling.

CHAPTER 11

Cool Green Water

Civilizations have died without water, hamlets never grow to cities without it, nor do boys grow to men without it. In fact, history has proved that in the days of early settlers, there were roughly two groups not concerned with life-giving water: those whose homesteads were near the lakes and streams, and those who frequented the saloons.

Thus it was in those early days in this high plateau country that tent cities were strung along the river and lake banks.

One of the ads enticing newcomers quoted this delightful notice:

FREE HOMES FOR YOU IN OREGON

No Crop Failures No Blizzards

No Sun Strokes   No Drouths

Some rode trains and bounced on a hardwood wagon seat for hundreds of miles, took one look at this dry side of the mountains, and went back, sore fannies and all. Others got a homestead or a timber claim or two, toughed it out, and built the country.

But the elusive water is knit into the heart and sinew and bedrock of this land. Seldom does it break the surface in springs; more often it had a lava cap of some 200 feet guarding it.

For several years, the Deschutes Rivers and Tumalo Creek in the Bend vicinity were the drinking water sources. About 1916, the big mills started and the usually clear and cold Deschutes was getting a one-two punch from them. Pitch and floating bark forced the issue of ditches being drawn off above and below the hamlet. An opportunist by the name of Lucky Baldwin made his living by hauling and peddling good water from house to house and camp to camp, selling it by pitcher, pail, or barrel when this problem arose.

The Swalley Irrigation Ditch, having whiskers historically, was drawn off below Bend before they had a drinking water problem, however. It was used for crop irrigation and for filling cisterns of residents who had a different problem — no water at all. The canal was started in 1899 by members of that family and two or three others.

Two separate central Oregon irrigation ditches were blasted through lava, one east to Powell Butte for that (eventually) good farming land, and the other north to Redmond.

Third in seniority was the Arnold Ditch, which is tapped at a particularly beautiful spot upriver of Bend, at Lava Island. This is the one that took care of part of the polluted water problem. A unique feature of this ditch was its engineering. It was laid out in its entirety by a man with a 15¢ pocket level. This remarkable man was Mr. Weist, who later laid out a subdivision of Farewell Bend called Weisteria. Until 1966, Mr. Weist's old family home was a fine example of early-day building with native stone. The city fathers missed an opportunity to save or preserve it when it fell victim to an already overcrowded service station expansion. Mr. Glen Slack, still a resident of Bend, worked for Mr. Weist in many capacities throughout that construction, recalling most of the details intimately.

The recent lava flow covered much of this inland area and springs were scarce. As the settlers moved inland to the east, wells had to

Jim Benham, pioneer sheepman of Laidlaw, and Charles Swalley of Swalley Ditch Company in Bend, 1910. Both men have landmarks named after them. (Al Moore)

Opal Springs in the Crooked River Canyon quench the thirst of all of Culver and much of Madras. The springs are still used and piped in for drinking water. (McCoin photo)

be sunk. And in this corner of the state where there is no known shortage of lava, "sunk" is hardly the word to use. In spite of cinders, pumice, malipai, and blue-hard basalt, dug they were, and single-jacked, and loaded, and shot. Windlasses were put together with what could be bought, borrowed, and begged. With such primitive equipment and obviously greenhorn methods, no fatalities or injuries, except one, marred the march of water holes across the desert. This one death came to a professional well-driller. His partner, Mr. Sachrey, gave much interesting information on the history of high desert wells.

Many wells were witched or dowsed. The going rates for digging then — $1 a foot for the first 500 feet, $1.50 for the next 200, and $2 thereafter — broke some of the families when drilled.

It was just that simple — and sudden.

Typical of that kind of thing was a traveler going to Burns who offered to dowse for water at one homesteader's tract. With his fork in hand, he circled, criss-crossed, and finally started up a hill near the house. About 100 feet higher than the prevailing level, he stopped and predicted water at about 80 feet.

At 80 feet, the driller hit a channel — of rushing air. He continued to drill. At 1,050 feet, there was no water, no money, and no homesteader.

These witchers were fooled many times by air channels in crevices and crevasses because they, too, make a static flow the witchers claim to feel.

Dickerson's Well, still listed on desert maps used by deer hunters, had quite another ending.

Manning Dickerson brought his family to the rim of the desert in 1913. They picked a spot about midway from Sand Springs and Aspen Flat, east of the recent Aspen Flat 20,000-acre fire. Mrs. Dickerson tipped her hand in calling it "the dream well," and finally told the story with a little coaxing:

"We came to the sageland and built, but had no water. We had to go four miles north of the house to a place called Pumice Well. The liquid was milky, poor for drinking, and unfit for lather. As we had two little ones, we used lots of it, but melted snow was better than it was.

"I became so discouraged with this, day after day, I broke down and cried. That night I had a dream, and it was so vivid that I woke up from it and then woke my husband, too.

"I had walked to a spot away from the house, looked down into a shaft, and could see water bubbling up like a fountain. It looked to be about 20 or more feet deep.

"The next morning I walked over to that spot and said, 'Dig here.'

"Edward Hethorne helped us dig, but we were leery of our project because we had heard of others that had been dug by hand 100 to 150 feet deep, and no water.

"We dug several days until we neared the 16-foot mark. I called them in for dinner. They went at it again after eating, but my husband had hit one good lick with the pick and he let out a yell that could be heard to Fort Rock. I ran out, looked down, and the water was gushing up exactly as it had been in my dream."

When we look at a map of the landmarks and wells scattered around the desert, this one will always have a little more personality than the rest.

The few springs that flowed also dried up from the decline in annual moisture. Others stopped, more spectacularly, from earthquakes in the California-Nevada region. Two of them, on the Dick Rody place and the McBroom ranch, stopped simultaneously. The latter rancher looked up the well-drillers, Schaeffer and Sachrey, who traveled the desert with a trailer to live in. They were booked up a year ahead, so they continued their rounds. Just to a year, as they packed and headed the rancher's way, he met them and happily told them his spring had started flowing again.

Other newcomers foolishly dynamited a small flow, trying to increase its water output, and ended up with nothing.

Many people today, and then, debunk witching; but where water is scarce, the dowsers hold a prominent spot in the water picture. Others have an open mind on the subject. The desert east of the Cascades has produced wells from 20 feet to 1,500 feet,

Pines, Dunes and Fossils

The Lost Forest, midway between Frederick Butte and Christmas Valley, is a sector of the desert that has quite a stand of fine ponderosa pines and shifting sand dunes. While there are two springs at the edge of the dunes, a well was dug there while it was being logged off shortly after World War II. In the digging, the men went through several layers of fossilized sea life in the form of snails, sea shells, and various fish bones.

The size of those yellow pines seems to attest to the fact of a good water table in the vicinity. Again, some of the Indian authorities say that this whole area was once under water because the size of the squaws' "bread boards" — matates or mortars — indicates they were so large they were hauled from one campground to the other by boat or raft. They were too heavy to be carried any other way.

most of them witched. The general level of the plateau doesn't vary much, so the water table must. Here is where the dowsers pay off.

Weather also affects the water table of a country. Many are the testimonials of weather change in the past half century. Earl Small, of the Silver Lake district, recalls seeing that lake seven miles long — today, it is a marsh. In the same area, John Crampton told of winters with a 30-inch snow cover; it is years since anyone has seen that. East, towards Burns, Jack Dribs remembers that the sleighs were in use month after month in earlier years.

Again, out on the desert, the Sherman family kept weather records from 1911 on, for 13 years. Rainfall averaged 15" to 16" at first, then slowly dropped, until today the average is 10" to 12".

Then, as the snows subsided, many ranchers left that land and that occupation for another.

This same kind of testimony came from settlers in the Sisters area at the very foot of the Cascade Range.

Mr. Caldwell recalls the winter of 1904-05 when there was four feet of snow on the level at Whitaker Holes, east of Millican. Another late fall, in March, brought two feet of snow.

George and Arvilla Murphy recollect about 80 springs in the Hampton Butte territory when they first lived there. Van Lake, a neighbor, told of five springs on one 80-acre piece he bought from the former "horse king," Bill Brown. But as the years passed, some flows stopped.

If the residents of this vast lava region are protective of the meager water supply, most have earned that feeling.

It must have been with this in mind that the soil conservation people pulled and capped many of the wells already in use during the drought years. Several of the long time residents had various comments on the subject. Perhaps typical is Dave Cody, who pitched a tent in the Brothers district in 1916 and has "bounced a horse off almost every rock from here to Wagontire since then." He said, "I know of at least 16 places to find water, but let 'em find it like I had to!"

Mrs. Ray Hethorne remembers their hauling water barrels seven and a half miles by team, and in the winter melting snow for washing clothes and dishes. "We saved water for so many years, I still can't stand to see it wasted!" she opined.

Mr. Johnson, who ran the Millican stage stop for many years, carried two pails a day a mile and a quarter each way, walking, when he first hit that country. Later he had good luck with a seven-foot shaft he dug that yielded five to six pails of good water until two of the neighbor's bulls got fighting and caved the well in. The flow never returned, and the 408-foot well at that town was finally drilled.

The incoming homesteader must have been impressed with the lack of water. Horses were 15¢ to 25¢ per head to drink, and a barrel was $1 to $1.50, depending on where you were.

To show how water etched itself in the memories of settlers, the Paul Riedells retraced, 50 years later, their trip to the Hamstead Valley when one of the horses was feverish from a cut. "It drank five times as much as the other one whenever we stopped

Across from Drake Park, 1910, Bend. (Kelley photo)

Oh, That Precious Water

Walt McCallum, of the famous Horse Ranch of Fort Rock, spun a tale dealing with the lighter side: "Whoever came into our neck of the woods stopped by for water from the spring down over the rim from the mountain mahogany. This one afternoon, a couple of sandsnipers came by with their rig and a couple of barrels. The horse was balky, and they were green. After filling up, they got down the lane a ways, and he quit on them again. Nothing worked. As we sat and watched, they held a conference, and soon had dry rabbit brush and dead sagebrush piled under the critter's belly. They lit it, and as the flames leaped up with a happy crackle, the noble steed, with admirable reflexes, gave two jumps forward, putting the wagon bed over the fire. The air was blue with smoke and references to that horse's lineage. Naturally, the barrels were used to put the fire out, but much of their outfit was lost."

to water up," they said. So water was a serious business.

Curiously enough, animals played a role in the discovery of some springs and water holes.

At the site of Old Collver (Haystack), the father of Mrs. Osborne was riding east, heading toward Grizzly. He saw wet prints coming from a hole close by, made by a badger. He dismounted, scooped a small basin in the sand, and it filled up immediately. He built the Osborne home a short distance away.

Again a badger was involved in the discovery of Wet Weather Spring, south of Bend some four miles. Here the teamsters

Bob P. Johnson came from England to homestead in the 1880's-1890's at what is now the west abutment of Haystack Dam. (McCoin photo)

had to skirt the huge lava flow that spewed out of Lava Butte and at one spot blocked the flow of the Deschutes River, pushing it westward. An unknown family heading for Rosland, all uphill and a tough grade at that point, saw a badger scoot away, his hide glistening. They stopped, scooped it out, watered their team, and thus Wet Weather Spring was born. The railroad bed partially covers it now, but occasional deer hunters run across the small seep that breaks forth in wet years.

The well-known Sand Springs known to hordes of deer hunters and former cattle and sheep men lies southeast of Bend. Here, where the ponderosa pines start giving way to juniper and sagebrush, Mr. Weaver opened it up to use because of a coyote. In his ride through this bleak, waterless section, he saw a desert pup busily digging. He dismounted and stole quietly ahead to watch the proceedings. Shortly, the coyote stopped

to drink. The spring was gradually enlarged, lined with rocks, and fenced.

Another source of the elusive substance opened many rides ago is still used by desert travelers. "Water was water, whether from a horse trough or a cow track." This was the succinct observation of one old-timer. This may have satisfied the men, but not always the horses. Johnny Pausch said, "When we hit the sulphur springs at Pringle Flat, the horses would never drink there till they had muddied up the water with their feet; we drank it as it was."

The scarcity of water on a ranch was measured by whether you could take a "two-week bath" or a "one-week bath." A copper boiler or galvanized tub was filled and set in the sun in the morning, and by afternoon the victim could hop into a warm tub of water.

Emil Van Lake told of a trip to Pine Mountain he made with his brother some 20 miles east of their ranch. Their chore? To select a fine, blue-skinned, dead but standing ponderosa pine. The blue specimens were solid. The brothers needed watering troughs for their livestock. Cut into 10-or 12-foot lengths, the logs were drilled with a long wood bit in several places from the top in a V shape to the bottom, 2/3 of the way through the log. They next took live coals and dropped several into each opening, then made the rounds with a Model T tire pump to get them fired up. In roughly 16 hours, the burned-out logs were ready to cut into and clean out. An axe and adze finished the hollowing job. Two that I saw in 1963 were still in use.

The watering troughs at the Niswonger stage stop in the Powell Butte vicinity had a tin cup hung there for pay. If all hands were busy with meals, feeding, or horseshoeing, the teamsters put their money in the cup, no questions asked.

Other Powell Butte residents told of some wells in that area over 800 feet deep, and no water. Old man Sheelley witched and claimed of an underground river's being in that land.

Before closing up shop on wells and water, there is another water source that has a unique personality, and it is none other than Bend's source. We get our water out of a glacier on Broken Top Mountain's east side.

From there it runs down into Crater Creek, is channeled for a ways, then drops down into Bridge Creek. Near beautiful Tumalo Falls, 12 miles west of town, there is a water setup from which it is piped into town. If you ever go west to look it over, be sure to look for the family of water ouzels that come back each year to raise their brood of young there. The caretaker will point them out to you.

Laidlaw top center. Pickett Island is where horses were kept overnight for the stages in the early days. (Ted Becker photo)

And what of the future of the Deschutes? Some 98,000 acres of desert lands are presently being irrigated from its flow to the east and north of Bend. The Bureau of Reclamation ditch alone is 65 miles long, carrying its flow beyond Madras. True, there are grains, certified seed crops, alfalfa, potatoes and more, raised from normally dry land. But the river can only take so much drain-off for irrigation purposes. And as the population pressure grows and people demand water, where will it come from? Rivers larger than this one have dried up completely from irrigation and domestic uses. Look immediately below Bend in July and August where the Deschutes "flows" and visualize its future if Redmond and Bend's population doubles or triples, which they are sure to do.

Looking to that time, what group, agency, or local government will have taken steps to save the river? At the minimum, the underground spring flows entering it below Redmond to Warm Springs will have to be measured to ensure a healthy river now and 50 years from now.

The bulk of this desert land receives 8 to 10 inches of rainfall annually.

Through the awesome depths of geologic time, less than a dozen major plants have evolved and stayed on this desert. Sage and rabbit brush, the junipers, bunchgrass, chamise, coyote berry, mountain mahogany from the green and the cover.

God put Mother Nature to work to select

Stauffer family and friends. This town which once even had a post office, is now a ghost town on the high desert. (Brookings photo)

and reject. When the dateless process was perfected, the antelope, mule deer, the sage grouse, the various rabbits, the skinks and blue-tailed lizards, the hawks, bobcats, owls, coyotes, and rodents had been selected as the residents of this land.

Yet today, man with his limited knowledge and experience has the effrontery to challenge and disturb this pattern of perfection.

Sagebrush is being sprayed with poison. So man kills not only sage, but desert sparrows, mice, insects, and also, indirectly, the larger birds and varmints who feed on the small-fry. Sage is the mainstay of antelope and the grouse.

When man is through piddling around, what will he have?

It might be a good question for the citizens to ask when they tamper with the lands we own — the government lands of Oregon.

Operations in the same direction have been applied to manzanita in the foothills, with the same deleterious effects.

Tapping the desert water table that can never be replaced fast enough to hold its own

is hardly agriculture progress. The cold, the drying winds, the frost, and the extremely short growing season make these projects marginal.

Man, in his brief stay here, has added to the desert perimeter by overgrazing, overplowing, and by the removal of soil-holding plants.

The deserts of the world grow larger each year; the one east of the Cascades is no exception.

CHAPTER 12

Fish Life

The pinions of the geese singing their northern flight heralds the mysterious calling of men upriver to feel the tug of fish on line. This unknown, unseen quarry pulled them irresistibly to the waters then as now.

The two Deschutes rivers were their standbys then, and few of the lakes as we now know them were used as fishing spots.

So it was that those little-known and little-seen jewels of lakes, East and Paulina, lay cradled in their pristine glory in Newberry Crater devoid of fish until 1911. That year, two separate plantings were made in a pilgrimage to that high, quiet mountain, to leave a leaven of life there.

The first wagon trip by four-horse team included a State man, name unknown, Grover Caldwell and a brother, and Bill Hollinshead. Their cargo? Thirty-five ten-gallon cans of fingerling trout. Grover called them steelhead.

For several years, Bend was the end of the line for the rails slicing south, so the fingerlings, or fry, were hustled off a car and onto a large wagon. The teams, men, and precious burden took off on the dusty, lava-lumped stage road towards Paulina Prairie.

The three men rode all night, taking turns filling one empty can and dumping the aerated water into the others from time to time. Squeaking harness leather, slurping water, and clacking wheels punctuated by the steady drum of horses' hooves broke the still of darkness. About four in the morning, the weary contingent pulled into a homestead at Paulina Prairie. Lee and Burt Caldwell were waiting with fresh and eager horseflesh to shuttle the load on to the crater's lakes, a tough 18 miles, all uphill.

The party crossed Paulina Creek where the road in does today, but swung to the left and followed the ridge from there on. It was dusty in the lodgepole and yellow pine country, but dripping snowpacks cooled their passage the last few miles. (Paulina Peak is just short of 8,000 feet high). Mule deer bucks, horns in velvet, crossed the primitive road the Caldwells had chopped through a few years earlier, stopped to stare, and picked their way carefully among the thickets so as not to injure budding antlers.

All but three cans were emptied into Paulina, the first of the twin lakes. The remaining three were rowed across eastward to the far shore in a boat of unknown vintage. Here the men labored with a can apiece over the old Indian trail connecting the two lakes to dump them into East Lake.

Later that year, another plant was made by another State man along with Mr. Pittman and Mr. Shintaffer of La Pine. Pittman's six-year-old boy made the three-day trip with them, a day up, one there, and one back. They too followed the road cut along the ridge.

In later years, Shintaffer tapped the hot springs lying close to the southeast shore of East Lake. There, each visitor to that primitive health spa had his own private galvanized tub and pump. No less than Irvin S. Cobb and his party spent a day at those hot springs at the tail end of a bear hunt in this area. While fire destroyed the facilities scattered around the springs some years later, it was from these small beginnings that the later reports blossomed. Today, fishing abounds all summer at this justly famous Newberry Crater.

Originally, some other lakes, like East and Paulina, were untenanted with fish. Elk Lake was bypassed for Horse Lake, a much smaller

"Fish Trap" at Pringle Falls

One of the heavily fished spots on the upper Deschutes was the "fish trap" at Pringle Falls. Indians still used it when the first white settlers moved in. This constricted passage was blocked by small rock dams in the evening, and by morning dozens of two- and three-foot Dolly Vardens could be speared or netted. This writer was shown snapshots of fish held above a man's belt, touching the ground. That redoubtable fisherman, Claude Kelley, told of a 42-incher he saw "way back when." Some liked 'em smoked, some liked 'em salted, done on the spot. One family spent two days here every fall to salt down two barrels of fish for the winter. But the log runs down the river knocked this fabulous angling hole out of commission. Above, 1910. Below, 1921. (Kelly photos)

neighbor. Devils Lake was fine for giving worms a swimming lesson, but nothing else. Today, it is planted with trout. Mrs. Zumwalt of Sisters, claimed her favorite as being Suttle Lake, nestled aside the Santiam highway.

River fishing came perhaps a little earlier than the lake angling, mostly because it took some exploring to find all the mountain lakes. But even the names designating the two Deschutes rivers have changed through the years. The old-timers referred to them as the East River and the West River; now, we often hear them called Big River and Little River. To keep the record straight, Big River, West River and the Deschutes are one river, the larger of the two, and East River, Little River, and the Little Deschutes are the other, the smaller.

At nearby La Pine, Bill Hollinshead took his two boys, Dean and Chet, to the Crane Prairie-Snow Creek country one fall for a winter's supply of fish. The boys' job was taking care of the horses while their dad fished. Dean recalls their arriving about midday and by the next noon having a 50-gallon barrel filled with cleaned, cut, and salted-down fish, all over 16 inches long when caught.

Some 50 miles north downriver, a Redmond angler named Jess Tetherow was fly-fishing the Cline Falls section of the Deschutes. A market fisherman, he was selling his catches to a Chinese restaurateur by the name of Tye. The trout were packed in weeds and moss, boxed, and shipped by stage three times a week. Jess, who knew fly-fishing at its best, named some of his favorite patterns. They were Professor, Queen of the Water, Black Gnat, Grizzly King, and Brown Hackle.

The community fish fries, starting in 1902

Fish Facts

Bend's Claude Kelley recalled a certain trip upriver when the morning was dipped in sunlight. As the water had a slight chop to it, the fish took almost any pattern, and when the action had slowed by 2 o'clock, he had tallied 108 trout, releasing all but enough for a mess. Then the limit was 125, later dropping to 75, 65, and 40.

This catch was from a Davis Lake wagon trip in 1911. (Slick Raper photo)

Cline Falls on Deschutes River near Redmond in April 1916. The town of Cline Falls is now a ghost town. (McCoin photo)

in Bend and held for several years, had the finnies furnished by the three Triplett brothers. A one to two-stint with their tackle at the present Drake Park site did the trick. It was common knowledge that some of the folks ate so much fish at these affairs, that they had trouble pulling their shirts off the next day or so. Something like dragging an army blanket over a barb wire fence, it was.

Another duo fished the very primitive country of Davis Lake. Slick Raper and Chet Hollinshed hauled their catch back to Rosland and dumped them into the watering trough in front of Bogue's store.

A favorite stunt of the men staging it on these jaunts was to wrap their home brew bottles surreptitiously in green, moist corn husks for the long wagon trips. Thus packaged, the delectable contents rode safely on the primitive roads and kept cool until dunked in the icy waters of the snow runoff in those foothills.

Bill Linster, a descendant of one of Bend's pioneer families, also talked fishin' — this in

spite of his being helplessly crippled by arthritis. He spoke enthusiastically of the early-day angling and said he believed local fishing became steadily worse as the man-made fish traps became clogged, broken, neglected. He suggested their repair and renewal as a starting point to return to those days he so fondly remembered.

Many then as now preferred Tumalo Creek because of the small, firm-meated trout it harbored. It was one of these trips west that brought the discovery of Tumalo Falls. Hugh Dugan and the Hayes Loops took the first known picture of that falls in 1918, the day they found it. Today, it is perhaps the most popular close-in spot for picnics for the seven months of the year when it is free of snow. It lies about 15 miles west of Bend.

The settlers were a lusty breed, and active. Many were the float trips down the Big Deschutes from Crane Prairie to Benham Falls.

Some of the known river-runners were Ted Becker, his brother, and his father. They made five trips from the primitive high country of Crane Prairie and Wickiup, then

Cline Falls on the Deschutes River

Post card below was on back of this photo.

completely untouched, to Benham Falls. The Beckers were a pioneer family of Laidlaw. Four of the Van Allens, Bill of Bend, his dad, and J. F. and K. E., with "Tom" Sawyer, also of Bend, made several runs. Steve Steidl, of the early-day family here, and Otto Store drifted it. Peter Beasley and Jim McCoy were also mentioned, but of the others who no doubt floated it for game and fish, their names are lost in the river's mist.

The run was 70 miles long, with two portages being necessary above Pringle Falls because of huge logjams. Most participants built rafts in the far, upper country, but the Van Allens used a canvas boat, portaging it when necessary. The rafts were sometimes lined through tough places. The stalwarts slept in any of the trappers' cabins handy to the river. The trips combined adventure and wild meat for the winter's larder.

Ted Becker recounted seeing a rare sight that would shake members of the Audubon Society today. A large flock of flamingos were flushed one trip. Ted said they were large, pink-feathered wading birds. No others come to mind answering that description.

One perilous passage was a narrow gut of water at Pringle Falls, slick but vicious. In

Peter Beasley and Jim McCoy hunted near Pringle Falls on the Deschutes River, then floated down with catch. (Becker photo)

Davis Lake catch, 1911. (Slick Raper photo)

those days, it hadn't been dynamited wide enough for the log floats. Boulders, black and water-rounded, choked the swift passage. The current pulled three bold hunters into the chute when they elected to run it instead of taking the unholy job of portaging their gear and game. They soon learned that danger and delight grew on the same stalk. The raft upended, losing seven deer and dozens of ducks and geese. All of the salted fish, the men, their rifles, shotguns, blankets, and tarps swirled out of sight in the mad water. Several rods below, three scared, cold, and bruised men fought their way to safety to spend a thankful night in Jeff Billeau's cabin. In June and July in that high country, the wind cuts like a hunter's knife. This was in the chill, crisp weather of the hunt.

On other trips, not so venturesome, families loaded sleeping gear, Dutch ovens, home-canned goodies, and fishing tackle into their wagons and Model T's to fill hardwood kegs and barrels or crocks with salted-down Dolly Vardens and other cousin-fish. The aforementioned Fish Trap was the usual destination.

Where low-flying planes stock today, it was different in Jess Tetherow's day, in 1921. He and a buddy worked for the Fish Commission, snowshoeing fish eggs to the high lakes, over late spring and summer mountain snows. The eggs were boxed in containers about the size of a cigar box, loaded on a sort of toboggan having two staves like the hounds of a wagon. "One of us was behind pushing and the other in front pulling on a stout rope," Jess recalled. "The loads ran about 500 pounds. We took to the snowshoes for the last high ridges where the drifts lay deep."

Other methods used were by alforjas (saddlebags) and saddlepacks, on horses, up mountain trails where unnamed alpine lakes lie ringed by mighty hemlocks and firs. Many of these footpaths were first cut by migrating game such as deer and elk in changing seasons. The Indians, the early trappers, and mountain men knew them and tucked them in a back corner of their memory for their backcountry wanderings. Next the Model A Fords and Jeeps opened them still

more. But today they are again shut off to all but horses and foot travelers, as they once were. Much of this has been set aside as primitive areas, to be preserved from now on. It is a fine move.

The State of Nature

Today, more than ever before, we need the profound depths of the wild to lose ourselves in, to retire to, to hike in and nestle down to a well-earned sleep as we give ear to the night winds. For, as man has progressed, nature has receded. No one knows this better than the dedicated anglers.

In central Oregon, for decades, the settlers drank of the Queen of Waters, the *Riviere des Chutes*, as the French named it. The lumbering inevitably changed the fishing on the length of the river. Too, bridges were built, and dams. Fish ladders, once effective and helpful, became clogged, broken, and rotted. The years passed and outboards came in, leaving oil and gas residue filming the water. Fishing pressure grew and limits dropped.

Motors grew in size and noise, inevitably and inexorably. Roads intruded more into the wild places where they were reached once by backpack and foot. Blacktop made them enhancing to the most citified sportsman. Less work hours and more leisure time spelled yet more fishing pressure.

High dams chop off age-old fish runs being replaced by some efficient (but some not so efficient) substitute fish ladders. Irrigation ditches took deeply of the Queen's liquid strength. Today, below Bend, she is a pitiful remnant of her former nobility and beauty. Her waters are perdiocally filled with roach.

This is not only the dismal story of the downfall of our Queen of the Waters; it is repeated for every river from Cape Blanco to Cape Cod.

For a few thousand years back, give or take a few, men have been fishing. Men who are otherwise gruff and hard-bitten sit back and quietly savor the beauty of nature. If there are some of the elusive finnies to bring back, this is an added dividend. Then the water-skiers hit the horizon. Roostertails, roaring outboards, pounding waves, and the roil of their washes beat the fishermen's senses. Right in the middle of these far removed outdoor groups are the peacemakers. They wear the uniforms of the Fish and Game, Wildlife, or Forest Service men. So lines are drawn, ropes strung up, buoys floated, and off limits signs scattered about the lake. No more is dropping a fly or trolling a lure the simple act it was 15 years ago.

Again, elderly Waltonians are rankled at having eight-power glasses prying into their every move. Others have been arrested for a leaving a line in the water while they scurried up the shore for more wood for their warming fire.

Youths, with a creeping scarcity of ways and places to give vent to their exuberance in urban America, have taken to water-skiing with a vengeance. So lakes that were relatively unused a few years back are bright with the scattering of colorful boats. Somewhere in this "no-man's-land" of nature's waterways lies an uneasy peace. Perhaps it is that one lake will be solely for fishing, another for skiing. Whatever the solution, the grounds must be policed — for garbage and all violations. The waters are fast becoming a dumping ground, as thousands use them day in and day out, all through summer. Somehow we must mature enough to stop defacing this land we have inherited. Would a $500 fine for garbage tossers be the answer?

CHAPTER 13

The Indians

The United States government and the Warm Springs tribe set up a reservation at the present site in 1855. At that time, the tribe gave up claim to all lands between the Cascades and the Blue Mountains of eastern Oregon, and also some of their Columbia River lands.[1]

The tribes involved were the Warm Springs, the Paiutes, the Teninos, and the Wascos. In return, they had 464,000 acres in the Mount Jefferson area, from the junipers along the Deschutes' west bank as part of the boundary, along the Metolius River as another boundary, and on west to the big fir and yellow pine stands near the foothills of Mount Hood.

The Indians have come a long way. The selling of their timber interests to private companies has brought a measure of prosperity to the tribes. The Indians themselves own and operate the plush Kah-Nee-Ta Hot Springs Resort, recently renovated and enlarged. There are increasing numbers of their rank in Central Oregon Community College in Bend each year.

On the whole, the Warm Springs tribe was always friendly and helpful to the government in any of the latter-day skirmishes.

The outlaw Indian, Paulina, much remembered in landmarks here, met a private destiny of his own. Claude Vandevert told some of the story. Claude still lives on the well-known ranch on the Little Deschutes. He has a rifle involved in that encounter. A relative of his, J. H. Clark, had a 45/90, model 1863 army rifle he carried with him that day and used on Paulina and his cohorts. As no ballistics expert ever extracted spent bullets from the renegade, and two other men were shooting also, it could have been the weapon that felled the self-made chief. Mr. Maupin has that distinction according to most historians, though.

Today, Oregonians talk of going to Wickiup, meaning Wickiup Reservoir, to fish. Another Wickiup, though, lies at the foot of South Sister. It is the little-known Wickiup Plain, to the west between the mountain and the timbered hills tumbling down into the valley side of the Cascades. While the two sites lie only a scant few miles apart, throngs visit the former and only a handful of hardy hikers and hunters know of the latter area.

Early settlers recall seeing the teepees or wickiups set up at the Wickiup Reservoir dam site before it was flooded out. The long poles used remained there year after year. Other places such as the Devil's Garden sector, near Fort Rock, had circles of lava rocks outlining the foot of their tents.

Two other Indian encampments mentioned were along Paulina Creek and the jack pines south of Wickiup Reservoir. Hair rope used to secure the tops of the poles was found by one central Oregon oldster near Crescent while riding herd; according to reports, it was judged to be over 100 years old.

Hollinsheads, Harrises, Moffits, Steidls, Smalls, and Caldwells recounted the habits and customs they observed in their contacts with the first Americans.

"In hunting," Dean Hollinshead said, "they strung out a line of six or eight, and bucks and does, willy-nilly, were shot as they were jumped. The men gutted the animals; the women generally dragged them in. For

---

[1] *An Illustrated History of Central Oregon*, p. 699.

some of this work, they used a travois, but this device was much used in their travels as well. The smaller children had their feet tied underneath the ponies' bellies so they wouldn't fall off, and they traveled many miles in this manner," he said. Another person mentioned that the Indians invariably traveled at a fast trot when on the move and that it was quite hard on the horses.

True nomads, the Indians were, always on the move. South for plums at Summer Lake, west for huckleberries and fish and to the low desert to follow wintering deer herds, to any of the inland villages where they traded for hides or cloth or necessities in season.

"It used to take six hours for them to pass on their way south to pick wild plums at Summer Lake," someone said. Another recounted, "They trotted through our fields in a cloud of dust for over an hour going north or south, to and from the game fields."

Whenever the Indians camped, a favorite game was gambling with two deer horns or pieces of bone, one plain and the other marked. This pastime could also be seen in later years at the Deschutes County Fair in Redmond, in the Indians' annual camp there.

Steve Steidl told of their camps at Bend's present-day Pioneer Park, aside the Deschutes, and of seeing the women rubbing rotten wood into the buckskin hides, hour after hour. Others were smoking deer skins or taking them from under water where they were softened before scraping. Steve recalls a large camp west of the river at the Gilchrist footbridge site strung to the west as far as Century Drive. "My dad bought ponies from them when they camped at Pioneer Park," Steve said.

Most women settlers were frightened of the Indians, and many of the kids were, too, although most could give no valid reason why. However, one recalled the Indian women's habit of calling their barking dogs to them by "Sic! Sic!" and thought the dogs were being "sicced" on them, so they became frightened.

Freda McDaniels remembered the Indians coming to Tumalo Creek to cut willows for smoking meat as well as getting the supple reeds they needed for weaving baskets. "They would trade huckleberries for fresh

Vandevert photo of their homestead on the Little Deschutes just below Rosland. This building still stands.

meat at dad's butcher shop," she said. "I was terrified, but my brother, Butch Clark, used to like to go down to their camps and listen to them."

Walt McCoin remembered the Indians partially drying huckleberries on blankets in the sun so they wouldn't crush so badly in their baskets looped over the horses. Hugh Dugan recalled seeing Mrs. Hayes Loop, an Indian, putting heavily sugared fresh berries in covered jars and turning them twice a day so the syrup ran through them. If kept in a cool place, they remained fresh for many days. The McClays of Redmond told of Indian flour, much used for bread when they were youngsters. It was a mixture of white and corn flour, or meal, made into Indian bread.

Of all the people talked to about the first Americans, Mrs. Galloway of Redmond knew them and numbered them more intimately among her friends than any other central Oregonian this writer has met. She had many gifts given her at deaths of various members of the tribes, some of them rare items seldom seen today. She had baskets woven of squaw grass, and many of twisted corn husks. Some of this corn husk work is so fine that 20 rows to an inch is common in their texture. An indication of the tedium of this work can be measured by the fact that only three to four rows compose a full and long day's work. A coarse bag had one-quarter-inch strips; a fine one had four to five times finer strips. The third layer from the kernel made the toughest husk. One strip, in weaving, makes four turns only, but it is pieced so well, once joined, one can't see where.

For the coloring of their various work, tribes swapped paints, but never gave up their color secrets. Some dyes were made of crushed roots or bark, others from colored earth extracts. Some known ones are juniper bark boiled in sheep's wool for yellow; alder bark yielded a kind of blue; black walnuts crushed and steeped produced a type of brown; burls from red fir baked for a few days supplied a type of red; and certain berries such as cranberries furnished a brilliant dark red, a type of magenta.

The corn husk bags were very useful. Even though they were beautiful with designs, some were 20 inches deep, hence useful and long-wearing, too. The Smith River baskets, used for children, had two and three sizes, from birth to two weeks, and correspondingly larger for older children.

For their beadwork, the Indians wanted Czechoslovakian beads, since they were the best, they said. Formerly, these were always secured from traders.

Another one of the Indian crafts, rapidly disappearing also, was porcupine quill work. Such work was chiefly put to use on war bonnets, although in later days it was sewed on miniature gloves, moccasins, and purses. The Indians loved their children, so these originally were made up for little girls' playthings. Now they are sold as souvenirs.

Mrs. Galloway made moccasins right along with the Indian women, although she admitted her first attempts at gloves left something to be desired. Doeskin is used for gloves, while the neck and the back, generally from a buck, is used for moccasins. When finished being tanned, the leather is white in color, but by smoking with apple wood it can be turned brown to blood red. The hides are watched carefully during this process. They are sewn in a cone shape, small at the top, placed over the smudge of a fire that is not allowed to flame but only smolder. Even the bullethole is sewn and hidden in using the hides.

While steps are being taken to preserve all

East or West Side Artifacts?

Most of the bowls for mixing grain, seeds, berries, and whatever were worked and hollowed out from the start by Mother Nature in a river bed. Another feature distinguishing these rock bowls here from their counterparts found in the valley is that ours are round-bottomed, or with a slightly pointed bottom for sitting in the sand, while many in the valley have short legs fashioned on them for holding in the slick mud.

the Indians' primitive arts and crafts, few are left who know how to practice many of them.

Little mention was made of pottery in this part of the west, and this skill is not plied nearly as much here as in the southwest. This much was mentioned by Mrs. Galloway.

"Mud and fresh horse manure were mixed for the mortar and colored with rotten wood of 'certain mountain trees.' " Only this seemed to be available for any of the pottery formulas for the central Oregon tribes.

Tule mats were one of the most useful items the Indians made. Besides all the utilitarian uses they found for them such as rugs, sleeping mats, and windbreaks in the winter, they were used for weddings, dinners, and ceremonial affairs.

For the annual "root festival" held each year, each of the several families of Indians had a certain plant to get and bring back for the celebration. This tradition was handed down through the families from one generation to another. Some got blue camas, others cattail roots and so on.

Of course, the mortars, bowls, and Indian breadboards used as pivots for ranchers' gates in and around Fort Rock were artifacts unearthed from another age far removed from this century.

The wide variety of points, awls, and tools made of colored agate, streaked obsidian, and jasper are from the same age period. This is the opinion of most Indian authorities, but other evidences point to this too.

The Sonny Joanis family found an arrowhead of black obsidian, at the edge of the Lava Butte lava flow. Its tip, for about one-quarter of an inch, was melted back and curled from the intense heat from the molten material. The remainder of the point, the ears, the edges, and taper is in perfect condition, unharmed by the heat. As this flow is reputedly about 2,000 years old, it would date the obsidian points found there as being before that eruption.

In speaking of the tools and wares of this earlier age, N. G. Seaman, author of *Indian Relics of the Pacific Northwest*, observed that obsidian, a type of natural glass, permitted an extremely sharp cutting edge, and thus was highly prized for this reason. The tribes traveled for many miles to get to sources of this material, or traded for it with other tribes. There are many known sources of obsidian, but a large circular area around Prineville would encompass good digging ground.

Seaman also observes that "spearheads" were seldom that, but were an edge put on a stick to dig roots. "Spalls" were chips off a larger piece of obsidian, to be formed into something later. Seaman even tells of chips of obsidian or rock being used to entertain small children: "When a papoose was left in its cradle a bent switch was placed at the head to bring the end above the baby's face. Two or more of these pieces were tied together, dangling from their centers in such a manner that the least movement caused them to strike together to make a tinkling noise. The same principle is used in the Japanese wind bells."[2]

A close scrutiny of some of these points will show the incredible delicacy of their craftsmanship.

But cruder work of a different age and different materials is also encountered. In the Lost Forest area of the sand dunes were found many extremely heavy breadboards. These were of a flat shape rather than the bowl type. Authorities reason these were so far back in the early history of this western section that this region was under an immense inland lake or sea. These large flat rocks were so heavy that they had to be transported by rafts from shore to shore, and could not possibly have been carried for everyday use by any other means.

The Fork Rock-Christmas Valley region held other interesting finds besides the nomads' tools and weapons. The Paul family of Bend found a skull with a small fragment of a hole in the forehead. A careful search revealed the arrowhead lying underneath it where it had slid out in the passing years. The skull was judged to be that of an Indian, a female, who was about 30 years old at the time of death.

Another unusual find for the weekend archaeologist is gaming stones. They mostly are about the size of a peanut, but this writer once found one larger than a bowling ball, and perfectly round. The small ones are round, or flat and oblong. A close examination will show small chip marks on one side and perhaps a bevel or chamfer on one edge. These marks are worn smooth from the many hours of shaking or passing them from one hand to the other. The stones are mostly black, but not always obsidian. Another find we made while sage hen hunting was about two dozen of the small stones in a four-foot circle.

Outdating even this age of tools could be the huge knife which Dr. Oglesby, of Fossil, found in 1884 near Mary's Peak in the valley. It was partially exposed under granite. It was an incredible 18" long, 3" wide, and 1½" thick along its back.

The doctor knew an Indian chief in the coast region and, on one occasion, saved his life when he was attacked by a grizzly. As a result of this, the Indian revealed to him their legends and histories and told him tales handed from father to son for untold ages. One of the narratives was of a tribe that came from the ocean with "big stone knives" and killed many people as they slept. It was Dr. Oglesby's belief that the stone knife he found was one of the knives described by the chief.[3]

And so the settlers moved in.

The Indians were split up into groups, placed on reservations, many times in "unwanted" areas. But some of the land was rich in minerals, timber, grazing land and scenic beauty. Bands of nomads had called it

---

[2] N. G. Seaman, *Indian Relics of the Pacific Northwest* (Portland, Or.: Binfords & Mort, 1946), p. 127.

[3] *An Illustrated History of Central Oregon*, p. 1097.

Indian Pictographs: Still Not Understood

Indian pictographs are another fascinating aspect of Indian culture. Wordforms of the Aztecs, the Mayans, the Egyptians, and others have been deciphered. The Dead Sea Scrolls dealing with the Essenes and other little-known peoples are becoming more of an open book. And yet the Indian pictographs seem to remain an enigma.

What of the Oregon pictographs? Are they game-hunting boundaries? Are they ancient treaties between warring tribes, or just the outpourings of talented primitive artists? They are a part of Oregon history that go largely unexplained. It would be a useful project for dovetailing unused grant monies at one of our universities. The sites containing pictographs could be visited and photographed in color and studied in the unhurried atmosphere necessary for this work.

Many of the old-timers know the locations of such writing but are loath to reveal them because they have, along with most of us, seen the known ones defaced, marred, and destroyed by vandals. A few known ones are about 25 miles out on the Burns highway; at the Devils Lake lava flow west of Bend are some more. An extensive assemblage of them is in the Lakeview area. A known collection of locations would be welcomed by students.

their home for centuries. They had lived in the infinite sounds of the past for generations. We would be naive to say that this richness should not have been developed.

So the tribes were fought, harassed, betrayed, cornered, and put on reservations. The minerals were first scratched, then gouged out by tons. Trees, untouched for centuries, fell in great swathes, first in the north-central states, then in the Oregon country. Prairie grass rolled out of sight in great furrows, leaving soil to be planted. Fences were stretched, and that was the last, great defeat. Wildlife diminished, and newcomers such as cows, chickens, and sheep replaced them.

The white men marched across the land with no less an imperialism than was used by many other countries in their civilized glory.

We did differ from them in some respects. Today the tribes are being guided by government agencies in many directions. They are being encouraged to seek their independence whenever possible.

And now their forsaken crafts, practiced for endless moons, should also be preserved. Whatever of their culture that can still be retained should be gathered and documented.

This last is the least we can do for these diminishing peoples. Somewhere out there in the past lies their one last encampment. They once stood and listened to the drum of bison hooves with a solid contentment, knowing they would eat tomorrow. Their papooses played in the dust of their teepees. They knew the seasons much more intimately than we know them. They felt the moods of our mountains and deserts and seashores long before we came here. Because this, too, once was their land.

CHAPTER 14

Cures

Sixteen-year-old Elmer Douglas was tramping a steady clip across the sageland heading west over Horse Ridge, towards distant Bend. He thought maybe he would get a ride at the Millican stage stop, but no luck. Hours later, he hove into Bend to look up a doctor.

He had been bitten by a coyote, and it could have been rabid. The townspeople directed him to the office of the pioneer Dr. Coe. The practitioner examined him, asked some questions, then started the wheels turning to get the lad to Portland for the rabies shots he needed. The necessary funds were lacking, so the medic started touring the streets of Bend — we had two then — asking for donations. When he had nearly enough, he put in the rest himself, and shipped the boy off on the train. The treatments saved the boy's life.

In those days, a doctor's functions transcended the dispersion of pills, the setting of bones, and the performing of operations. He was a family advisor, philosopher, psychologist, father confessor, a dispenser of candy, and a healer by laying on of the hands and, at times, by his very presence.

The doctor had to know how to harness a horse, diagnose a case correctly in a matter of minutes in a serious situation, know which bones lay where without an X-ray or having to go to his books to be certain.

Besides this, he had to know all the intricate turns of vague roads and lanes for those ever-prevalent night calls.

At times, he took chickens, venison, vegetables, or milk for pay. But meanwhile, back at the ranch, what do we do? What do we use?

One of Mrs. Mosley's boys was thrown from a horse. He fell across a barbed wire fence and cut his throat terribly. He made it home because the jugular was not severed. "I poured turpentine into a bowl, dumped a cup of sugar into it, and mixed the two into a paste," said Mrs. Mosley. "After cleaning the wound as best I could and gathering it together, I pulled a clean bandage of the mixture tightly under his chin and tied it in back of his head. Four or five days later, when we could get away, we drove from Ashwood to Prineville where the wound was examined and found to be healing so well that nothing further could be done."

Onions were a great home remedy. They were boiled, fried, steeped, or sliced raw for flu and colds. Onion syrup was used in most homes for coughs. Honey, whiskey, and lemon were added at times. "If we wanted flavoring for such dubious liquids, we used horehound," one person added.

When George Murphy laid his foot open with a sharp axe on his Hampton Butte ranch, he was miles from help. He held his foot under icy spring water and sewed the edges together. "It healed up nicely," said George.

Dean Harris said, "We always had to have a cup or two of hot mullein tea every spring. It was supposed to be a blood purifier." Plenty of watercress salad during the summer served the same purpose. George Lynch said his mother always saved any bear grease when the family or friends got a bear. This, mixed with various things such as mustard or an onion concoction, was rubbed into the chest for influenza, pneumonia, or colds. Heated turpentine on flannel was another favorite. A muscle linament was the white of an egg whipped in — you guessed it — turpentine.

Kerosene was reported to have been good

A Malady Widespread In The West

In several months of talking to settlers, various symptoms were given of one common form of fever, generally found in men only. It is unique insofar as the healthier the victim, the harder he is hit. It is simply known colloquially as hunting fever.

As in most diseases, the symptoms vary in individuals. It mounts slowly, increasing in fervor and tempo until the patient is talking to himself. He wanders around idly, bumping into things, as if he had double vision. Again, he appears to be looking at an object or person, but at the same time seems to be looking through the thing observed. It is as if he were staring at a faraway, legendary place, while dripping from his chin. A close scrutiny will enable the examiner to see that the victim is definitely glassy-eyed.

In the cases where the fever comes on in a matter of minutes, the cases are baffling, because what triggers the disease mechanism is unknown. It can be a frosty morning with the elusive smell and atmosphere accompanying it. It can be an unusual sound, like a lone flight of geese, that turns this normal, sensible family man into a gibbering idiot. He appears not to hear his wife or see his children. He pokes around strange corners of the house, in the closets, in the basement, picking things up and laying them down, muttering to himself while sorting and piling up odd bits of trivia.

A piece of rope suddenly takes on a new significance. The smell of a tent can send him into a chorus of a forgotten song. Endless sessions with his knife and sharpening stone drive his family to distraction. Strips of paper and bits of severed hair samples lie at his feet.

Maps are a definite threat to the welfare of the victims of this disease. The sight of one will send him scurrying to some table, unrolling the charts, making notes, marking, folding, in all manner of employment while a stream of endless mumbling falls from his lips.

When affected by this disease, bachelors of known gentle disposition forget to chase women and take to kicking at dogs and swearing at small children. In extreme cases, they have been known to curse their favorite bartenders. Sulfas and the various myacins are all ineffectual. Hoppe's #9, if given shortly after the initial onslaught, is very soothing. But ironically, a whiff of this while the fever is mounting will make some men nuttier than a fruitcake.

The feel of the cold steel of a gun barrel will mollify most unfortunates struck low by this dread disease. A ramrod and a gross of cleaning patches will ease and mitigate the mental stress encountered. Such temporary measures keep the men occupied during the crisis. Again, box of rifle or shotgun shells to tumble back and forth between their hands will suffice for others.

It is best to keep children away from the stricken one, not because the disease is contagious, but because the victim is in a state of mental instability. He might be led around by the hand like a two-year-old, or again, he might let fly a string of invectives mighty unsuited to childish ears.

The terminal point of the illness having been reached, it is inevitable that the sufferer should take a trip into areas where there is much ozone. The sagelands will do for some; the manzanita and cutover lands will do for others; for stubborn cases, the rough lavas or the dense jack pine thickets are necessary. Burned food, wet clothes, long hours of violent exercise, and chilling weather are all very effectual as a partial cure during this period. But in one in a thousand cases, these measures only serve to heighten and prolong the fever.

If in this state, the man is liable to much profanity. He never shaves, his clothing becomes disheveled and filthy. A prolonged rain or fresh snowfall adds to his bad habits. He may eat only one meal a day, and never wash his dishes.

But a lengthy stay in this state will eventually burn the most stubborn fever out of him. All that is necessary is a clean shave and a bath upon his return home. In a week, after much bragging, he should be ready to take his rightful place again in society.

The town of Stauffer turns out for a 4th of July celebration. (Brookings photo)

for appendicitis, toothache, croup, corns and bunions, and scalp cleansing.

Pumpkin seeds got rid of worms in children. A flaxseed meal poultice was used for boils and abscesses. Alum was used to quench bleeding. Ringworm was treated with a strong solution of tobacco leaves.

One remedy for sore throat given was a piece of fat bacon sprinkled with black pepper, and tied around the throat. Surprisingly, no one mentioned sulphur and molasses among home treatments.

Earl Small was thrown from his horse and got a break, somewhere in the shoulder. They were miles from the home ranch and still farther from Silver Lake and a doctor. So his buddies got out their knives and whittled a wooden boot that fit under his arm to hold it in the right position. They cinched it down with a sling and Earl finished the riding job until he could get away some days later. No further work by the doctor was necessary.

When Dean Hollinshead got his arm broken, his dad took over the job as doctor, too. He split a shake for splints after setting the bone in place. A careful wrapping and the usual sling completed the job. The arm healed normally in every respect.

One other home remedy given, with tongue in cheek, bears retelling. It is of arnica, supposedly having wonderful curative powers. The concoctor of this homemade salve earned the name "Arnicky" as its fame spread. The story is told of his having just finished pouring a batch of it in jar covers and other shallow utensils spread on the back porch to cool and harden. A neighbor's dog passing by was intrigued by the strange smell and came over to investigate. The dog took six or eight swipes with his tongue at the strange mixture, but it had a vile taste, so he hightailed it home. The taste persisted, however, and the unfortunate animal took to licking his hind end to get rid of it. The healing power of that salve was so miraculous that this portion of his anatomy healed and haired over in three days.

The flu epidemic was persistent enough in its spread that it hit the most remote outposts. The breath of that plague left many dead at ranches or lonely line shacks.

In Bend, one lady recalled that everyone helped swab throats in her neighborhood with the usual standby — turpentine. "People wore masks when downtown, delivering milk at houses, or coming in contact with one another," she said.

It was smack in the middle of this epidemic that Dr. Thom of Silver Lake found himself in 1918. Mrs. Thom said he treated 115 patients in a period of 18 days.

On his return to the office each night, it was Dr. Thom's habit to sit at the top of the stairs and sort out the medicines and potions to be dispensed the next day. One night, before he finished his task, Mrs. Thom heard a thump and a clatter. Exhaustion had finally caught up with the good doctor; he was sound asleep at the head of the staircase while his wares had rolled down two flights of stairs.

As with all country doctors, Dr. Thom had a large territory to cover. Yet he had a remarkable record in saving those epidemic patients.

After things had quieted down a bit, he had a broken leg case clatter up in a wagon. But if a man can survive getting pitched out of his rig three times on the way to town to see the medic, and survive . . . the broken leg would seem to be of secondary importance. The patient lived but the horse got lame from the trip.

CHAPTER 15

Sourdough Talk

When the Antelope fire destroyed all of John Silvertooth's old-time collection a few years ago, a superb array of that country's history went up in smoke. But another item of a different nature was also burned in that fire.

"Sourdough" Welsh had a book of small talk he had compiled while sitting around in Antelope's only bistro, and in it he had sourdough recipes he had wangled out of the itinerant sheepherders, camp tenders, roaming cowpokes, and drinking ranchhands. They totaled up to some 40 different sourdough formulas. They were all lost in the fire.

Another person who collected these rather unusual recipes was Mrs. Walt McCoin, who had over two dozen of them. Some of them were very old.

John Scott Sr. got his sourdough starter from a Reedsport man who had it supposedly unbroken for 60 years. If my memory serves me correctly, Dave Cody's starter was carried over from the same batch for 16 years until his place burned out.

One settler said when the pantry pickings got tough, and they ran out of flour, they had a sourdough recipe that used "middlings" — the one and the same middlings used for livestock feed. It makes sense. Anyone who has worked around a barn doing chores has probably grabbed a handful of that cattle bran to tide them over until supper time.

Earl Small opined, "I was a good sourdough man, but I'd prefer getting wood or water to cooking the biscuits."

Another dozen or so of the old camphands had reputations that went far beyond them for mouth-watering biscuits.

To aid and abet these culinary experts, the Bend Mill made fine flour while it was in the business. This was from the dry-land, hard wheat from the Metolius and Culver country, and it was some of the finest grown. Some of it was hauled as far as 50 or more miles to the mill. Their "middlings" were so fine that many homesteaders used them as hot cereal for breakfast.

One lady told of the time she worked at the Redmond Hotel during the days when the irrigation ditches were being put in and the railroad was a going business. "I cooked, baked, carried water, and waited on tables for the many construction men there. We had one table we kept set and reserved we called the 'drummers table' — it was for the traveling men and salesmen."

She continued: "The cook was always so busy that one day I decided to help him. So I kneaded his sourdough bread, put it in pans, and baked it. When he came in, instead of smiling, he got so hopping mad, he quit! And this, with 100 men to cook for! Ray Covert and his brother, who took care of the horses and my husband all pitched in and helped me until another cook came. This took time because word had to be sent, a man hired, and then brought down from Portland."

Many were the unusual foods mentioned that people cooked, home-canned, or prepared for winter. Most ranches prepared their own sausage with their own homegrown flavorings, such as sage. It was put in five-gallon crocks and had hot grease poured over it.

Other ladies recall various methods of canning venison. Some of these were delicious. But the dozens of pints and quarts took their toll with some of the women. "It's been years, but I still don't like venison!" one said.

Sage hens were often used as the mainstay to build a meal around. People took the young ones when they could, but most all were cleaned immediately and soaked in soda water, then drained and fried.

"We smoked our hogs with mountain mahogany because it gave them a fine flavor," one man told me. Today, many local people ride to the edge of the desert each year to get this same hardwood for use in their backyard barbecues.

"I cooked anything the kids brought home in the line of game," a lady from Terrebonne told me. "This included porcupine. If it's fixed right, it isn't bad at all." Others told of eating bear meat, and, here again, they preferred a young animal. If fixed right, it is hard to tell from pork.

Elk were generally on the protected list for game animals in those days, but if the opportunity presented itself, some people brought them in for winter's meat. One such case had an element of humor in it.

"We were camped in the Irish and Taylor Lake country cooking up elk steaks on a late huckleberry trip," one man told me. "When the steaks were just getting done to perfection and the beans were being dished up, the country's only game warden came riding in, so we asked him to stay for supper. After we

---

Tales Untold

From sourdough to sour mash isn't too much of a jump, and it's too bad the bootleg stories all couldn't be retold, but most are too close to our times. If it were 50 years later, a book on this subject alone could be written.

---

were done eating, he lit up, and said, 'Well, I'm riding down over the side into Roaring Springs tomorrow to check on the elk herd. I 'spose you guys will be gone by the time I come back.' We were.

Among the seven saloons in Bend at that time, the Log Cabin Saloon had a sign over the bar that read *"No Whiskey Served Over This Bar Until Seven Years Old."* Whether this meant the customer or the whiskey is not known.

One gentleman told me that he had a neighbor rancher that was having a tough time making a go of it. He went in to bootlegging, made very good money, bought a better place and cattle, and now is a big rancher, respected by everyone.

Only recently — in the fifties — a forgotten still was found not too far east of Bend in one

The Bend Flour Mill Company, 1916. This building burned down. (Kelly photo)

Picnic, 1911 (Kelley photo)

Raper Saloon in La Pine, 1911.

A Bend group picnic in 1910. (Steidl photo)

Sheriff Roberts, on left in front of car, and deputies with a day's haul of bootleg equipment from the high desert. (Roberts photo)

Desert still, uncovered in the late 1940's. "Liquor was fine tasting." (Gladys Workman photo)

Bootleg Days. *(Roberts photo)*

of the desert's many caves, and when the product was sampled, it was found to be infinitely smooth. The years had been kind to it.

This was one that Sheriff Roberts of Bend missed. But while in office he had a total of 234 stills to his credit.

Another tale was told by a grizzled veteran of the cattle country. "I was in town and heard about a two-ton truckload of bonded whiskey coming in from California," Grover said. "Later, I overheard a lawman talking to one of his deputies on the party line. They were going to try to intercept the driver at the county line. His cohort was told to try to raise $300 to dicker with. I hung up and rode out to get to the driver before they did, intercepting him between La Pine and Bend. I sketched a

High desert still. (Gladys Workman photo)

Sheriff Roberts and deputy. (Roberts photo)

map of a roundabout way to The Dalles through the desert. For many years afterward, this lawman eyed me suspiciously whenever we met in town.''

There was also many a rocker in the hinterlands that never rocked a babe. They were used to age desert dew to a passable perfection.

The copper vat, piping, and spirituous paraphernalia it takes to brew a batch of red-eye or white lightning was recently found in a remote area between Antelope and the John Day River. Any wandering hunter of arrowheads, birds, deer, bottles, or birds can still find the remnants of stills.

If you want to pinpoint your search, perhaps Dale Tussing could have told where his marking rock covered three quarts of good Canadian whiskey. The general area is two to three miles south of Brothers.

Sourdough Recipes

The making of sourdough bread all depends on your yeast, as it is a yeast similar to light bread, only it has a tart taste, and is made with soda. A true sourdough never has baking powder in it.

I make my starter with commercial buttermilk now — it will start sooner.

The real secret in any sourdough recipe is knowing just how much soda to put in. The soda tempers the sour taste. However, too much soda makes your batter brown and streaked.

One more caution: According to the old-timers you can only use the pancake recipe on a calm day—they're *that* light and fluffy!

Sourdough Yeast Starter

2 cups slightly sour milk, in stone or glass container

Add flour to make a medium batter. Put in a warm place and stir often. In a few days it will ferment to a yeast. When using, take out the amount needed to make the size batch of bread wanted. Add more milk and flour for next time. Stir often. As it rises up, stir it down. Fresh milk from the cow is the best.

Bread

2 cups of starter
Scant tsp. salt
1 tbs. shortening
¼ to ½ tsp. soda, depending on how sour yeast is
Enough flour to roll out into biscuits (not too much)

Sit in a warm place to rise a little.

Pancakes

1 cup starter
1 cup flour
1 egg
½ tsp. salt
¼ tsp. soda
1 tsp. melted shortening

One lady adds the soda when she puts them on the fry. Another adds soda when stirring them up.

Sourdough Cake

1 cup sourdough
¾ cup brown sugar
1 egg
½ cup butter
½ tsp. soda
½ tsp. salt
Flour to make a stiff batter

Let rise all night where it isn't cold, and bake.

Sourdough Cookies

1½ cups brown sugar
½ cup shortening
½ cup butter
3 cups quick rolled oats
1½ cups flour
1 tsp. cinnamon
½ tsp. cloves
½ tsp. allspice
1 tsp. soda
2 cups sourdough

Chill and roll out and bake.

Sourdough Piecrust

1 cup starter
½ cup shortening
¾ tsp. salt
1/8 tsp. soda
½ tsp. sugar

Flour enough to roll piecrust.

Desert kitchen of the "ZX" BBQ Ranch. (Dr. & Mrs. Thom)

CHAPTER 16

Livestock

A gruesome account given in one of the historical books covering the sheep and cattle wars gives us an insight into how high feeling ran during this period:

It was in one of these (rock and brush) enclosures that a band of sheep, most of which belonged to Benham Brothers (of Farewell Bend), was corralled on the evening of February 3, 1904. No sooner had the herder corralled his sheep than five masked men rode up to him, emerging from a hiding place nearby . . . compelled him to stand with his arms up and his back to the crowd while they placed a sack over his face and tied his hands. He was then compelled to stand by a juniper tree, while, with rifles, pistols, knives and clubs, the clubs being juniper limbs about four feet long and the size of a man's wrist, the masked men proceeded to slaughter sheep.

"There were in the neighborhood of 3,000 head in the flock. It was just getting dark when the slaughter commenced, and it took nearly all night to complete the job.[1]

Johnny Pausch, who ran sheep 11 years for Bill Brown, the Horse King, and many years for himself, thought that much of that trouble was caused by things other than overpasturing. Drifters (or bums as some called them) caused much of it. Some of them had 600 to 800 head of sheep, owned no land, used water when they came to it and pasture as well; they paid no taxes. None of this set well with either the legitimate sheepmen or cattlemen.

Another method used by sheepkillers was to fan out behind a band of 1,500 or 2,000 and run them over the edges of cliffs to their deaths. Those that weren't killed outright were later shot. These men used unshod horses in their killings so they could not be

Crane Prairie spring cattle crossing. (McCoin photo)

---

[1] *An Illustrated History of Central Oregon*, p. 827.

Jim Benham's sheep shearing crew (before 1910). In the ongoing battle between sheep and cattle men, many sheep were killed.

tracked. The hundreds of wild horses running the high plateau covered all evidence.

It was a messy business, with no holds barred. But there were other killers of livestock, too.

The first three or four winters in the 1880's were listed in the annals of the early stockmen as terrible killers. March of 1906 was yet another — after an extremely mild winter. In the three terrible winters mentioned, some lost from 50 to 90 percent of their herds. But in that March storm of 1906, it plunged down viciously out of the north, bringing snow and 20°-below weather that lasted for exactly two weeks. The cattle would water at the water hole at Pringle Flat and the cold was so acute that in a few hours the hooves were frozen to the first joint. The cattle would lie down and, in trying to get up and around again, would lose the first joint of their leg. Again, when the calves nursed, the moisture froze on the cows' teats so quickly and severely that they lost them. In both instances of frostbite, the cattle had to be destroyed. At that time, they were worth $20 a head.

It might have been that winter that Claude Vandevert recalled it got down to 49° below zero on his place on Little River.

Regarding price per head, when stockmen made a deal with each other in the spring, whatever ensued during the following months, they kept their word. Seldom was there a signed contract. A verbal agreement and a handshake sufficed.

One of these early stockmen was Joe Taylor. In 1898, he received the first grazing permit issued by a government ranger in this area. The government man was one of the pioneer Vandeverts. Taylor's grazing grounds are still marked on Forest Service maps as Taylor Burn and Taylor Lake. Another name in that area is a holdover from the summering of sheep there: Sheep Bridge was a plank run over the smallish Upper Deschutes, wide enough for one animal only.

Another cattleman who carved a chunk of the desert out for himself was remembered by a town of his name — Millican.

For many seasons, Johnny Pausch took 1,000 sheep for roughly 150 miles to and from summer pasture. The names and stopovers on the trek westward from his G.I. holdings to Irish and Taylor Lakes are partly unknown now, but a few still have a familiar ring.

The trip, starting in June, took one month up to his allotment and roughly three weeks back. The Price place, Pringle Flat, and Harney Holes were three of their first stops. They watered at a ranch about a mile north of Millican and came down what Johnny called Pine Ridge to the canal. The Griffith place was the last stop before hitting the highway.

"We hated that highway stretch," Johnny said, "because the cars always gave us trouble!"

The highway was paralleled as far as Harper Bridge and turned west to the old Fall River hatchery. They commenced climbing then and headed for Sheep Bridge, Brown's Creek, and on to the Elk Lake-Davis Lake road. The west side of this was Johnny's boundary for his summer allotment. The west corner was the Taylor Burn, then south to the Twins, back east to about the west shore of present Wickiup Reservoir, north to the Davis Lake point of beginning. Three fattening months were spent in this high, lush, green country.

A typical day saw the men and dogs up at daybreak to feed the sheep until about eight in the morning. Then the herder and tender came in for a hearty breakfast. The sheep bedded during the heat of the day. Then they moved out at about 4 p.m. and fed until dark.

Old cattle crossing bridge at Crane Prairie before it was flooded. Cabin was built in 1915. Photo taken 1917. (McCoin photo)

The Stanley cabin on Crane Prairie Reservoir site was used by cattle and sheep men summering stock in the 20's and 30's. In the fall they returned with the stock to Madras. Cabin was built in 1915. (McCoin photo)

"We ate another big meal before taking them out for the evening feed. All summer, we had mostly two meals a day," Johnny said.

He had many interesting comments on the seemingly prosaic duty of being shepherd to such an expanse of animals.

"We used two dogs, invariably dark in color," he said. "One dog was kept tied, because they are like kids. Two are always playing or showing off; one will work.

"There were about eight or nine 'markers' in a band, dark sheep to aid in counting or keeping track of them. There were also several belled sheep, to aid in hearing them in the brush or at night. When a small bunch wandered off or got lost or separated, they usually followed a belled sheep. Sheep like to follow a belled sheep.

"I preferred a part-collie, part black-and-tan shepherd dog instead of an Australian Shepherd. The Australians were a little rough on sheep, and their bites could hurt them. They were very good dogs, though.

"We had three pack horses and one saddle horse. Our stuff was stashed in five-gallon kerosene tins boxed up in alforjas, two tins to a side.

"The sheep liked to feed by a bright moon, but we had to stop that; we had to have some time to sleep," Johnny said, grinning.

After the practice of poisoning coyotes was initiated to keep those varmints under control, the dogs were always kept muzzled to protect them from eating the poison baits.

When it was a new dog's turn to help with the sheep and he was untied, he immediately held his head up for the muzzle to be put on. Then he went to work. The dogs were worked mostly by hand signals, but some were adept enough in their trade that they needed no commands.

Mr. Pausch told of the time a herder named Robinson was herding a band of Bill Brown's when they had to come and get him but had no replacement for him. Five days later when the men returned, the dogs still had the sheep in tow.

The Glass Buttes area was hard on the dogs' feet because of the sands being shot through with splintered bits of obsidian, the natural glass found in that area. In a few

Numa McCoin roping wild horses in a trap corral at Grandview in the 1930's. (McCoin photo)

days, their feet would get raw. Rawhide puttees were used.

Preceding the sheep by many years were the wild horses — "broom tails" as the buckaroos named them. From Millican to Wagontire, there were thousands of them when, near the turn of the century, some men counted them as a money crop.

That, indeed, they were, during the war years.

The bulk of the riders were running horses, not cattle. As some said, "It was a tough way to serve the Lord!" The riding chores were twice as tough and fast as riding herd on cattle, and it took many riders to run down a bunch of the knot heads. Seldom was it done by two or three riders because the horses had to be pushed until they tired enough to corral or keep bunched by riding them in a circle.

"We had to use .45's to turn the damn things before they ran us to death," said Grover Caldwell. Grover still has his sidearm, slick, shiny, and knicked from many years of use. He originally traded a mare for it.

Bill Brown's wild horse empire lay roughly east of Bend. Farther north, the McCoins, Osbornes, Reads and others were herding

"Bill Brown days", running and trapping wild horses east of Bend to sell to the government for World War I cavalry mounts.

bunches into the Willow Creek Basin. If this doesn't ring a bell, later it was called Palmain and eventually Madras. This area was near enough to the Warm Springs Indian Reservation that Walt McCoin recalled several Indians he rode with, all fine riders. Among them were Dave and Willie Ike, Tom Wanawert, Cane Bruno, and George Ritt.

"And we traveled, too," Claude Seeds said. "In one month I went south to Fort Klamath, east to Burns, and northeast to Summit Prairie."

Others getting into the act by grabbing themselves a handful of horseflesh were the Weavers, ranching on the Crooked River below Prineville. In the years of the McKinley presidency and somewhat later, they sold 1,000 head to the government.

In those days, there were no fences on the high desert for miles on end. But as more and more people bought land, pasture and feed had to be protected for their own stock, so the day of the fences came.

It was a pitiful sight, many said, to see the terrible wounds the wild horses got in running through them in headlong flight on their way to water or after being spooked by something. At full tilt, they were cut by them like a buzz saw. So the ranchers started hanging strips of white cloth on the wires to protect both the horses and antelope. The latter invariably slow down enough to crawl underneath the bottom strand, unlike the mule deer, who leap them.

Many of the early riders for Bill Brown, the so-called horse king, got their start in ranching from that financial assist. Two of these, Johnny Pausch and Grover Caldwell, later had large herds and spreads in that same desert area.

Grover recalls the time he rode four months steady, seven days a week for Bill, some days bringing in 300 head. "We would brand the colts, cut the studs, trim their tails the right length to help keep flies off the wound, and brand the famous horseshoe brand on each side of the jaw."

Men that Grover rode with were Frank and Sumner Houston, Van and Ray Ritter, Henry Carlin, Shorty Hoffman, Frank McCulley, Dave Cody (cousin to Bill), and Link Hutton. They had six to eight horses to pick from each day. The one-horse cowboy is strictly a myth.

Few recall today that the Hacklemans and Bill Brown introduced good-blooded horses into the desert stock to breed out the large head and other undesirable characteristics.

But as plentiful as horses were out there, Mrs. Nelson said homesteaders had to rope and break their own animals if they needed them for riding or freighting because few could afford to buy them. An incident por-

He sired 500 or more, 1910-25.

In the Silver Lake sector some 80 miles south of Horse Ridge, Earl Small's dad imported three jackasses, raised mules, and drove 300 of them to far-off Nebraska, around the year 1897.

Nearby, the McCallums at historic Fort Rock made a similar trip to Bly, California, and paid $1,800 for a huge jackass, above.

"For such a price, he must have had a fancy name," this interviewer suggested.

"Oh, he had a name alright," Walt sighed, shaking his head. "He had many names — all unprintable!"

This pioneer family was also in the freighting business from Silver Lake to Bend, and sometimes Prineville and Shaniko.

traying this fact was told by one: A rancher had to leave for three or four days on a trip to town and was giving his daughter final instructions. He warned her, "Now if anyone comes snooping around, SHOOT! But dammit, don't hit the horses!"

The Sherman's homestead out near the head of the Crooked River is in a lush section of the generally arid desert. They told of the "fall ride" and the "beef ride," and had many riders during the busy times of the year. It wasn't all work, though, and they told of the mornings when so many saddles were hidden by pranksters on windmill tops, in junipers, or in outhouses that they couldn't muster enough to ride herd.

One of the early ranch hands, Dave Harrigan, used to get a green rider in camp while the bunch was sitting around the fire and say, "Give me your knife, pipe, and tobacco while I cut me off a smoke."

Several said that there were better shows on cold mornings trying to saddle up than are seen nowadays in the good rodeos.

Occasionally, the ranchers took a postman's holiday.

The wild stallions had the nasty habit of stealing the choicest mares. When this went so far, the irate men got together and salvaged what they could by running the solitary stud's harems into temporary corrals. Many a surprised rancher saw his brand show up on a horse long since given up.

Even as late as the forties, strays with

Jennys at the historic "Horse Ranch" near Fort Rock. (McCallum photo)

brands were bringing $5 to $10 a head when returned.

Roy and Thurman Moffit, 12-and 16-year-old buckaroos, found life on the rangeland not always dull.

They were taking a bunch of cattle through Bend, heading for Long Prairie (now Paulina Prairie) at the turn of the century. When they were just a few miles south of town, one of the supply horses caught its pack under a tree limb, and that started things moving. That slab-sided bronc cut more tracks in the next three minutes than he had in the past mile. Round and round it went, bucking and backing in a circle, with pans, spuds, flour, jam, beans, bacon — everything — flying out of the loosening packs.

"Oh, yes, I remember," said Roy, "there was Tea Garden Syrup, too, lots of it."

In minutes, the horse had plunged and tramped the whole works into the ground. When the melee was over, they savaged a handful of spuds, beans, and dirt.

"On that same trip we left camp to see if we could get a grouse or two," the boys said. (There were grouse south of Bend in those days.) "We shot one, but about that time we saw a wild cow. We were bound we were going to milk her. After quite a scuffle, we roped her and got the job done, so we had a little milk for camp. But when we got back, the dog had eaten the grouse."

The Moffit boys started riding and summering cattle when they were ten years old. Old George Millican used to stay at their folks' place on his way to Prineville to get supplies. Roy said he remembered him as quiet, tough, and resourceful. That about sums up most of the early settlers.

So when Millican made a deal with the Moffits, selling them a bull out on the range near Sand Springs, Thurman got to go along. He was ten at the time.

As it can on the desert, though, it turned bitterly cold in a few hours. They got to the spring, and no cattle or bull. They scouted around, waited, looked some more, but finally had to build a fire to thaw out. They had nothing to eat, and spring water isn't too fattening. With just a saddle blanket to sleep with, they turned in as the long night dragged on. When you sleep cold, it is the

longest night there is. About daybreak, the bull came around, and tickled they were to drive him home. It was one rough trip for a ten-year-old, but this stuff is what turned them into men in a year or two.

If the trips were rough at ten years, they were still rough for eighty-year-olds, too.

Dave Cody made enough money trapping and selling coyote pelts to buy his homestead north of Brothers in 1916. In 1966, when I met him, he was still there. To help in getting some notes from that colorful character, this writer brought a car trunk of box wood for Dave's kitchen range, a five-pound can of honey for his sourdough biscuits, and a length of used rope. This last item, any rancher from Brothers to Boston can always use.

Both of Dave's horses had died during the winter. "One was 30, I know, and the other older still," Dave said.

"The old mare had been gone all winter, but came in during the spring," he continued. "I could see that she was sick. She stood and looked at me for quite a while, then she went and got a drink. She walked to the top of the west ridge, looked back again, and nickered. I said 'Goodbye, old girl.' I never saw her again."

Dave had tough luck with his lambs that spring, too, and lost many. It was the usual spring on the desert — bitter. All his dry wood was gone and his juniper pile was mostly of green stuff to nurse along for a fire. He had two blue tick hounds to feed and no dog food. His eyesight was not good enough anymore to go out and shoot rabbits as he used to, and both his horses were dead, so his riding was done, too. The batteries were down on both cars. He needed a tractor to work up the fields for the rye crop, but after pricing them in Bend and Redmond, found they were too high for his pocketbook.

To cap it all, Dave was running out of hay for his small band of sheep. It seemed that in 48 years the desert hadn't given in an inch or softened one little bit. It got its pound of flesh, and no one knew it better than Dave.

But this isn't the way it ended, nor have a 100 other such stories ended this way. Because Dave has neighbors.

Friends from nearby Brothers and adjoining ranches look in on him every few days. They bring him dry wood and work some of the big chunks up. They manage to save scraps for his hounds. A fellow rancher had been helping on the hay problem longer than most people know. Another will get a battery charged for him.

If someone told Dave he should move to town, he would no doubt ask, "Why?" None of the aforegoing reasons are enough. So Dave stays on to live on his beloved desert.

Other people put the same idea —the rough life — in words of their own.

"Our bedrolls were big," Mr. Small stated. "It took a horse to carry them. This was by design, not accident." The thin, dry air of the desert changes quickly from 80° in the afternoon to 20° at night. Earl told of one morning he and his buckarooing partner woke up to find a foot of snow on their blankets.

He summed his reminiscing up with the statement, "I would hate to get all my falls and breaks back again!"

One of the falls witnessed by a group of snickering cowhands in a Bill Brown camp was taken by the cook, a Frenchman. He got so mad he quit then and there. Grover Caldwell inherited his job, and got quite an apprenticeship from that incident.

"We used lots of venison and antelope

Wild and Mean

When the cattle drives were over, there were occasionally outlaw bulls left wandering the countryside. These became a menace to anyone passing through; when found, they had to be destroyed. Bill Parton and Earl Small had to go after one such animal bearing the Z X brand. The chore of apprehending this seven-year-old fell to them between Christmas and New Years of one year.

About the third day out, they found the bull — or should we say he found them. He charged them on sight, and both men were glad they had good ponies. These animals were huge. In those years, even the steers went until they were four years old before they were marketed. Neither man had had a chance to get a rifle before they left and they were armed with handguns only, so the men were skittish about any wild or uncertain shooting at an animal. With one man and horse acting as a decoy, the other eased up behind the bull and one of the .32's was emptied into him. The only outward effect was to knock him to his knees for a second or two before he ran off. By now, the men worked him into some big timber so they would have some little cover for the man decoying. Parton dismounted and hid behind a large ponderosa while Small worked the animal by him. It was touch-and-go for a man dismounted, but some close-in shots finished the bull off.

when we could get it, but had beef and mutton, too. I got to be quite a hand at biscuit-making that spell,'' said Grover.

Some of the stops of the Hanley and Brown cattle and horse camps were Glass and Hampton Buttes, South Sand Spring, Last Chance, Lost Forest, Fossil Lake, and Christmas Valley.

The Cal Shermans used the first known portable chuck wagon in their cattle ranch cooking chores — an ancient Buick touring car. It made many a bouncing trip in the environs of the upper Crooked River-Buck Creek sections.

''We had an oven that baked 45 biscuits at a time,'' recalled Mrs. Sherman. ''We used this rig on our June rides and beef rides.'' (To the uninitiated, the June ride was the drive to the cattle's summer range, and the return trip in the fall was the beef ride.)

Cattlemen of the Summer Lake region told of an affliction peculiar to that steep rimrock area bordering the lake. It was known locally by the stockmen as ''rickets.'' It was a stiffening of the cattle's hind legs experienced from being taken down off the rims to the lower Summer Lake range. If left on their own, the cattle never suffered from this trouble in the steep descent. But let a handful of cowboys ease them down off the slopes, no

matter how often they rested them or how slowly they traveled, the cattle stiffened up, lost control of their legs, and rolled down until injured on rocks or trees. Many had to be destroyed.

Not all of the range work was exciting or serious. The men had their fancy work for their odd hours.

They saved horsetail strands, or cowtail, used a jinny to twist them together, and put them into a hair rope. Riatas, nosepieces, buttons or rosettes, hackamores, and McCartys were made of varicolored strands from the animals. Others used raw-hide strips. Cal Sherman recalls seeing a beautiful 60-foot-long, hand-rolled rawhide riata, with honda. These were practical and were used for roping on particularly windy days because they were heavy.

Grover Caldwell many times saw Big Jake Winishut ride by with his long rawhide rope and wondered what he used it for. ''One day I saw him snaking an elk out of a canyon in the Roaring Springs country. I stopped wondering from then on,'' he said.

The McCartys had a peculiar use. Most cowboys of the desert had a particular dread of being tossed and having to walk to camp or water a hundred hills away. So the McCarty was tied to the hackamore, coiled up small,

Rolyat (Taylor spelled backwards) homesteaders south of Hampton and five miles north of Stauffer. 1915. Later called Brookings or Half-Way House. (Gladys Workman)

and shoved into the pants or shirt where it could be grabbed in a hurried unloading from a cantankerous horse. A skittish horse could be held with this, even after a man was thrown.

One of the old cowhands made an interesting observation about roping. He said a left-handed roper can't do a thing with a horse while lassoing, because the horse is always trying to get the rope on the other side of him. The man and the horse were always fighting each other. Which raises the question: Was there ever a good left-handed cowboy?

While it is not unusual today to see cattle summering in the mountain country west of Bend, it is not nearly as grazed as it used to be. Forestry officials and other government agencies have curtailed grazing privileges to prevent overgrazing. Johnny Pausch recalls a figure of about seven acres per cow per month when he used to summer 3,000 head in Taylor Burn.

While men like Johnny, Cal Sherman, the Hacklemans, Cofelts, Smalls, Harris, and others have large spreads now, or once had, there were lean years and long rides between for them. They started small, kept tallying larger herds, and bought out a discouraged neighbor now and then. They took what the desert had to offer and rolled with the tough punches. One day, they could do as one did when a group of hunters came to him for a hunt on his land.

"How much land do you own, mister?" they asked.

Holding out his outstretched arm in a long sweep, he said, "As far as the eye can see!"

But the world changes, even the world of cattle and sheep.

Cattle are trucked now from summer to winter range. They lose precious fat if moved too fast. The only thing the ranchers haven't changed or licked is the weather.

It is either too dry, or too cold, or too windy, or too rainy. One bent-legged character put it succinctly, saying, "It rained so much one beef drive, it would bog a snipe on a saddle blanket."

The smaller operators, in such weather, don't have enough variety of rims, draws, and broken ground for protection for their livestock during storms. And a discerning traveler passing through this midstate area will notice that most open buildings face east or north. He can deduce correctly that most of our "weather" comes in from the southwest.

The small rancher is disappearing. The huge land and livestock corporations are taking over. Outlying lands are being peddled off in one- to five-acre tracts at a very tidy profit, so profitable that the land comes too high for a farmer to buy and add to his small holdings.

So the boisterous cowpoke is fading from the scene, so full of snap he had to walk sideways to keep from flying. And good cowhands are hard to come by. The only thing he could shoo on a horse today is the flies. They don't know one end of a cow from the udder.

If a man can replace a blown tube in the TV set, weld a split in an irrigation pipe, or drive a semi, he might get the job.

The forgotten smells, gas fumes from the Model T truck, the musty ammonia-like fumes from the inside of a small barn shackled in frost and ice in winter, juniper after a desert rain, are not savored as they once were. We are three generations too late.

CHAPTER 17

Freighters

The freighters and stage drivers were a breed apart. Their runs were tough, lonely, and exasperating. Everyone moving into this new country was in hurry. The upstart businessmen had to have their supplies and goods on schedule. The newcomers were unused to hardship and complained at the dust, the mud, the eternal bumps, and the breakdowns. Few were complimentary about a ride on time, with a minimum of trouble.

The Bend Book, published in 1911, stated that there was a loss of one horse per trip by death or accident from Bend to Shaniko. And this was the average. Considering that these runs were made hour after hour, day and night, summer and winter, one begins to get the picture of the toll the runs took. In other words, on most days, six, eight, or ten of these animals were retired from duty each day, humanely or not, depending on the mishap. The writer of this same book told of passing 64 wagons hauling freight and people between Shaniko and Bend in one day.

Someone has said, "If there are two people in hell, one of them is a cold iron blacksmith." And these resourceful skinners all had to be one of these. Wheels fell apart, axels broke, teams ran away, brakes failed on Cow Canyon Hill. So they either sat or got some haywire or scrap iron and fixed things

Freight wagon from Shaniko arrives on Bond Street in Bend near the Pilot Butte Hotel in 1910. (Kelly photo)

Freighters amidst ponderosa pines.

The Shaniko to Bend freight team made many stops in 1910. (Roberts photo)

temporarily.

At such times, there was some vivid verbal ornamentation unsuited to tender ears. Then, as the drivers sat hunched over, with rain trickling down their necks, they dreamed of the next stop, of a warm room with the gramophone playing ''The Merry Widow Waltz,'' a hot drink to thaw the marrow, and a bull session with another skinner.

Then, just as today, when men got together they argued makes and models of their trade. Some of the wagons were Newtons, Studebakers, Rushfords, Mitchells, Bains, Yellow Fish, Winonas, Red Fish, Oshkosh, Peter Schutlers . . . . On and on into

the night, the freighters talked, and drank, and argued.

The freighters usually went from town to town; they went from Wenandys to Bogues. They traveled from Estebenets to Vandeverts to Tetherows, or from the Horse Ranch to O'Neils.

The stopover places were not always post offices; more often, they were livery barns where teams or mounts could be changed, fed, and watered. A boy could always get a part-time job harnessing, grooming, and currying. Many times, the boys slept in the hay to be handy during the night for odd-hour travelers. Such travelers tipped, same

O'Neil Stage Stop? (McCoin photo)

"Staging it" from the railroad south of Shaniko 1910. Up to the axles in mud. (Kelly photo)

Lee Caldwell outfit in front of Aune's livery stable in Bend, 1905. Caldwell ran cattle in the La Pine and Sunriver areas. Aune owned much of downtown Bend and had a feed store on Bond Street. (Courtesy Mrs. Austin Kaiser)

Gas buggy at stage stop in high desert. Note hard rubber tires. Probably 1910 or 1911 truck. (Brookings photo)

Gas surrey with fringe on top at Half-Way House. (Brookings photo)

Vinton Wray's Stage about 1918 in high desert. Note air tires. (Gladys Workman photo)

Turbine and gear for first electric power plant in front of J. A. Eastes building, now site of U.S. National Bank in downtown Bend. Arnold Shearer is on the horse and Ralph Dunn is in the wagon from Shaniko in this 1910 photo. The power plant machinery was installed on the Deschutes at the Newport Bridge. (Kelley photo)

as the day travelers did — some good, some poor, some not at all. Individual drivers used these facilities as much as the professional teamsters.

Some of these stops had sizeable investments and a thriving business. Bogues had a stock of several thousand dollars in a store, a 14-room hotel, and a livery barn with 20 head of horses for hire at Rosland, on the Little Deschutes.

Farther north, on the Big Deschutes, the Tetherow family had another of the larger stage stops. Facilities included barn, livery stable, blacksmith shop, and 20 wagons for hire with teams to power them.

The Niswonger stop in Powell Butte was known for many years. The Vandevert stop on Little River came before Bogue's place, traveling from Bend south. And the Horse Ranch, still so called, was the McCallum's freighting headquarters, just west of Fort Rock.

Evidences of the investments required to staff and operate a stage line were picked up from some of the old hands. One stage line that went from Antelope to Mitchell, a distance of 55 miles, was said to have required 18 horses for its operation. Someone recalled that a good piece of horseflesh ran

anywhere from $100 to $300. Mr. Whittaker remembered that ''Freight was a cent a pound from Prineville or Bend to Rolyat (later Hampton) and 'more' from there on east.'

And here a name causing much confusion came to light. It was Highpockets McDowell, and Highpockets So-and-So, depending on who was narrating or remembering a stage driver. After several attempts to pin the name down, the confusion was enough that the term was completely dropped. Then Mr. Whittaker, a farmer and teacher in the Pringle Flat area, also used it designating a teamster. He quoted the above rates and added that the inhabitants in this section thought that the prices were too dear to pay for having goods hauled. Hence they pinned the term ''highpockets'' on all the drivers on these runs.

The advent of a new stage connection was as newsworthy in those days as the announcement of a new air terminal would be today! ''In November, 1904, it was joyfully announced that Prineville was in communication by telephone with Shaniko and The Dalles, and had six stage lines running to Shaniko, Burns, Sisters, Crook, La Monta, Silver Lake, Mitchell and Bend. The total mileage of these routes was 476. A total of 26 offices were served by these stage lines."[1]

Not all wagons were single affairs, pulled by a mere team. Tandems of two huge wagons were common and loaded down with a system. Such terms as "leaders," "swing team," and so on mean little to us drugstore cowboys nowadays. But to take a few ton of furniture up switchbacks of the Crooked River canyons, or out of Cow Canyon, took much horseflesh and much skill on the skinner's part to add up to successful freighting.

Six- and eight-horse teams had their animals specifically named. The six-horse team had the "lead team," the "swing team" next, and the "wheelers" for the heavy pulling. The eight-horse teams were called "lead," "point," "swing," and "wheelers". One horse had to jump the tongue in a tight turn and then jump back into his rightful place again.

Some skinners drove by jerk line; some rode the left rear horse next to the wagon. Why? Because a horse is a better shock absorber than a hardwood wagon seat over a 40-mile run.

Periodically, the wheel sections (felloes) had to be soaked in almost boiling oil to preserve and tighten them. A shallow pan curved to fit the wheel was put under it while the load was raised and blocked up. Six or eight turns with a few seconds soaking at each turn finished the saturation. Water was also used for periodic tightening.

Curiously, of the many who came into contact with these men, it was a woman who remembered the charges for putting up teamsters. Mrs. Zumwalt, of Sisters, whose

---

[1] *An Illustrated History of Central Oregon*, p. 728.

McCallum's freight team arriving home at the noted Fort Rock "Horse Ranch" from La Pine and Bend. (McCallum photo)

Hotel Bend. (Slick Raper photo)

folks kept travelers, sheepmen passing through, and one-night-stand men quoted 40¢ for a single and 75¢ for a team. This fee included feed and water and the shelter of the barn.

These runs were not made by timid drivers, or the cargoes would never have gotten through. The skippers of the desert ships had strong hands and held from four to six sets of reins in them for hours on end. Cheeks like leathern flasks and squint marks deep from glare or wind-driven dust aged their faces beyond their years. But they had sentiment. Jim Toney, Joe Taggart, and others are still remembered by many women today because when they had little girls with pigtails for passengers, they were sometimes allowed to ride on the seat beside the driver.

One of these men, when he died a few years back, asked that the funeral procession make his run again — his last. So the cars drove slowly from Redmond to Prineville and back to Redmond. It was a fine gesture. It gave his cronies a chance to relive those years an hour, argue who first built on this piece of ground, and remember the name of the good-looking waitress who worked for a time in the old hotel.

Old Prineville Hotel. (McCoin photo)

Hotel Chrisman, La Pine, 1911. (Slick Raper photo)

Hotel Riley, La Pine.

McCallum's Horse Ranch near Fort Rock was an important stage stop on the Silver Lake, Fort Rock, Bend line. Shorty Gustafson and Dean Hollinshead ran this freight line with horse teams. The 200 foot well was dug by hand and still stands as a landmark. 1909. (McCallum photo)

Central Oregon Freighters

Marsh Awbrey	George Hobwood	Charlie Mume	Charlie Weaver
Frank Bogue	Bill Hollinshead	Jack Naker	John Weigle
Mr. Bransom	Dean Hollinshead	Mr. Nelson	Jack Wenandy
Bill Buckley	John Laam	Dave Rogers	John Wilson
Mr. Evans	Joel McClay	Jim Scoggin	Vinton Wray
Hinkler Ferris	Mr. McCoin (Walt's dad)	Mr. Sears	John Yancey
Mr. Gilbar	Highpockets McDowell	Charlie Solomon	Steve Yancey
Dave Grimes	Dad McEachron	Joe Taggart	
Jess Harter	Mr. Mason	Frank Tucker	

CHAPTER 18

Wildlife

To help us get an insight into the former game in this portion of the state, some pioneer writers made observations almost one hundred years ago concerning it.

"Jim and A. H. Marks, Uncle Buford's boys, were born hunters and this country was to them all that could be desired. Deer were plenty everywhere; not little runty white tails like they have in the Willamette, but big, mule deer, animals as large as an elk. Elk and bear could be found in the mountains; wild sheep on the high, rocky buttes; big grey wolves once in a while and coyotes everywhere."[1]

The year was 1868. And again:

"That winter was a busy one to all of us. . . . Sundays we washed and patched our clothes . . . we thought we had come with clothes enough for a year, but three months ranting around over the rimrocks and through the juniper trees after the mule deer had left us barefooted and naked. . . . Newt Bostwick capped the climax in the footwear line by soling a pair of moccasins with a piece of bacon rind. We all wore moccasins and before spring buckskin breeches and shirts."[2]

Another interesting story comes from this same source: "During the winter of 1868 the Vining cabin was occupied by M. B. Fry, now of Albany, whose chief ambition was to get up a race between a thoroughbred greyhound he brought out with him and one of the fleet-footed mule bucks that were then so numerous on our valleys and plains. But before he succeeded in this desire he made the grand mistake of turning his slim-waisted, long-legged racer loose after a mangy coyote that looked fully as hungry as his dog. There was an exciting race for about a quarter of a mile and the greyhound overtook the coyote who proceeded then and there to give it the worst whipping a high-bred town dog ever got. Then there was another quarter race back to where Fry stood in open astonishment, the greyhound in the lead, but the coyote a good second and every few jumps he would nip a piece out of the fleeing dog's hams. That race ruined the dog as a hunter, for from that day on Fry could never induce it to chase a jack-rabbit, and the howl of a coyote drove it under the bed. After that it pined away and died."[3]

In talking at any length to onetime homesteaders, the subject eventually got around to the desert dogs — coyotes.

Van Lake had this to offer, in a conversation with him before he died.

"I paid $25 and two hams to get my coyote recipe," he said.

"What was in it?"

"Oh, Russian musk — I sent away to get that — and it was expensive."

"What else?"

"Well, there's . . . ." Then he stopped. With a rising fire in his eye, he put his face close to mine and demanded, "What you want to know for? You plan on trapping?"

"No, I'm not going to trap."

But Emil wasn't eight. He was 83 years old and hadn't lived on his desert ranch for

---

[1] George Barnes, Prineville *News,* June 1887, quoted in *An Illustrated History of Central Oregon,* pp. 706-707.

[2] Ibid., p. 706.

[3] Ibid., p. 706.

several years; but no one was going to get his prized, and highly secret, recipe for trapping coyotes.

In those days, the little dogs even made the newsprint on occasion. This from a Bend newspaper of 1903: "A coyote walked Wall Street Tuesday morning, but kept well out of sight before guns could be brought to bear."

In 1916, there was a seige of rabid coyote stories making their rounds, with good basis. Recalling those days, George Murphy told of one coyote running through a large herd of cattle, nipping at their tails.

In another instance, a driver of Ferris Trucking, out of Bend, was making his run across the desert when a coyote leaped at him. He killed it with a lucky hit on the head with a ball-peen hammer.

A nearby rancher was attacked while working on his truck in his ranch yard. This coyote was killed with a hit from a monkey wrench.

Dean Harris told how a coyote chased Parton's dog right into the house during the rabies scare in the Summer Lake area. After several minutes of wild scramble, they killed it in the house.

While Mrs. Paul Riedel was teaching in the Hamstead Valley during those perilous days, a concerned neighbor loaned her his handgun to use while walking to and from school.

Another incident that happened at Riley, out of Burns, was witnessed by Ted Becker of Tumalo. A coyote had a terrified horse by the tail and the two were whirling around in a cloud of dust. Someone with a good eye and a steady hand shot the desert dog without hitting the horse or spectators.

Cal Sherman related how the different ranches fared in that 1916 rabies scare, when losses ran from three to thirty among their neighbors' livestock in the Hampton Butte sector. Families south of them lost up to 12 head.

In those primitive days, many people made their living or paid off their homestead by trapping coyotes. Some told of getting 25 to 30 a day, if their runs were long enough. One oldster got 50 of them one fall, bringing him $16 apiece.

While some people trapped coyotes for money, others trapped, poisoned, or shot

Joe Breeding of Lamonta, "story teller supreme." (McCoin photo)

them to stay alive in the livestock business. One of these was Johnny Pausch, former owner of the expensive G. I. spread. He remembers, with little joy, the years he lost 109 and 400 sheep from coyotes. He said that in earlier years a small band of sheep that got separated from the main band were all goners unless they were found in a day or so.

"After intensive poisoning and trapping started, the small bands were almost always intact until we found them," he said.

Some settlers got started in the cattle business from cash earned by trapping the little dogs. One such rancher made $700 in 14 days and used the money to buy six cows from Charlie Perry, a neighbor.

In the winter, the coyotes used the rabbit runways, and a grizzled veteran shot 13 of them from his kitchen window.

The little varmints were bothersome in the Powell Butte area too. A bachelor living south of Pancake Hill got a good buy on some 30 pullets. He let them run and in no time had more eggs than he could use, plus a plump hen for the pot whenever he savored one. When he took a part-time carpentry job

Mule deer buck. (William Van Allen)

in Redmond, however, the coyotes took over.

"It must have been at least two weeks before I noticed one day that my flock of pullets was getting thin," he said. "There were only 14 left. The next day I came home to see one smart coyote herding three of my chickens to a corner of the fence to trap them. I ran and got my rifle and bagged that one. When I skinned him, he was so fat from his chicken diet, he dripped grease. Then I got busy and put up a six-foot wire fence to put the birds in. I was getting a fire started for supper one night and came out to feed my pullets. There, halfway up that six-foot fence, was a coyote about to crawl over the top. I took my fist and hit him in the back and knocked him out."

A share of coyote stories told of the settlers seeing them partly or completely bald from scabies, a disease that hit the sheep herds.

The aforegoing is on the debit side, but it would be unfair to close out the books in this manner. The coyote is to the west what the loon is to the north country. His cackling laughter dropping off a rim will haunt the mind of the newcomer as well as the old cowhand. That wild cadence of sound has caused many people to raise up on an elbow out of their sleeping bags at some ungodly hour of the desert night.

One winter, Manning Dickerson made snowshoes for his trap run on his homestead and the outposts beyond. He trapped, poisoned, and snared. When the fur was done flying, he had 3,000 pairs of ears, at five cents a rabbit.

"We saved them, bundled them, and brought them in to collect our windfall, but they had run out of bounty money just the day before," he said.

Mr. Sakry, on his homestead south of Brothers, used the same methods to stack up his rabbits, but he saved the hides. The first batch he sent to Fromsteens Fur Company in St. Louis. He got 85¢ a pound. The second shipment brought 65¢, and the last lot dropped to 35¢. "I quit when it got that bad because I was staying up until midnight and later, skinning and stretching 200 or more hides night after night," he recounted.

Bill Stenkamp gave another method they used to deplete the hordes of bunnies eating the bottoms out of the haystacks until they fell over: "We took two-by-fours and drilled holes about an inch in diameter in them, then filled them with a mixture of salt and strychnine. We collected the carcasses each day, but one morning we found our six hogs out eating the dead rabbits. We knew dogs and cats could be killed from eating poisoned rabbit, so we waited that long night out, worried sick at losing our winter's supply of meat. I got up early the next morning and found those porkers fat and sassy as ever."

One of the Stenkamps also told how they raked the poisoned bunnies in rows with their farm machinery on a 3/4-mile stretch where they used grain and strychnine to thin the hordes. After being piled, the rabbits had to be burned.

P.B. Johnson, who ran the Millican store for many years, recalls that in the first years of 1911 and 1912 there were no jacks at all, just snowshoes and rock rabbits or cottontails. Then in 1915 they started coming in and year by year increased until the grain fields were overrun with them. It was during these years that the kids made spending money at 3¢ a rabbit.

Walt McCoin recalled the winter that he and his brothers killed 57 with a magazine full of .22 shorts while on a hunt on the Sell place near their home. On another drive in the Silver Lake vicinity, an unbelievable pile many feet long and six feet deep was the tally for the day's drive when clubs were used.

Several thousand rabbits were killed in this drive at Silver Lake, 1913. (Mrs. Thom photo)

Rifles were first used, but someone got shot so guns were forbidden by common consent. It was on one of these drives that some enterprising townspeople counted the critters and found they had bagged 7,500 wild hares.

Bobcats were another varmint the ranchers had little use for, but in the opinion of most, they were a cinch to trap.

Van Lake opined as how a bobcat was stupid compared to a coyote. He trapped 32 cats in one week. Another said he got three to one, in ratio, between bobcats and coyotes. Most used the same bait, but some shot a bird and hung the fresh kill over the trap.

While the ladies had little comment on trapping, several were emphatic on the cleaning of game brought in for them to cook. "The women didn't clean the game," Mrs. Hethorne said. "The kids or men who shot game had to clean it around most home-steads."

"If this were true nowadays," another oldster volunteered, "there would be less ducks and geese shot by these hunters."

Some birds didn't fall victim to birdshot but to blacksnake whips. The Harris boys and others in the Silver Lake area got proficient at cutting their heads off with this weapon. The sage hen of their day showed a decided lack of wariness. Yet their presence by the thousands was providential because they fed families unfamiliar with firearms, until they learned to use them on more wary game.

Hundreds of low-lying spots shown on early-day maps held water enough for nesting ducks and geese, Summer Lake being *the* bird country. It was here during World War II that a coterie of hunters saved up their gas tickets for a hunt there. The first scattered shots boomed across the marshes. After a particularly heavy barrage, there was complete silence, and a plaintive voice was heard wailing, "Come back and fight like a duck!"

Almost everyone of the old-timers talked to still had one or more of his original hunting artillery. Calibers seldom heard of now were standbys in those misty times: the 44/40, 40/60, 32/20, 40/82, 38/55, 45/90, 38/40, 33 Winchester, 35 Remington, and .22 Hi-Power and Hornet were named by the settlers.

Some of these vintage rifles had handcarved stocks of fir, apple, juniper, or maple. That these were prized and much used was obvious. Most were bright from lost bluing, knicked, dented, and scarred, yet the marks were honorable. These guns were the tools of their trade, along with the axe, and they were hung in a prominent place over a mantle or tucked in a convenient spot behind the door where they could be snatched in a hurry.

This next is for gun buffs only. Gus Schuman has in his possession a 50-shot group made at 25 yards with a Model 52 Winchester .22 measuring 5/8 of an inch. Even in these times, that is a remarkable group.

In speaking of their hunting habits then, Mr. Schuman said, "We merely wandered out of town in one direction or another to get our deer."

Right here in Bend, the Steidls, Tweets, and Sathers shot geese all year-round in what is now water from the mill to Mirror Pond.

The Weaver Boys' dad in 1916 told them, "Thirty-two years ago this winter, we did nothing but hunt deer. We took 97 of them to The Dalles for meat." That was the savage winter of '84, and what they didn't use their 45/70 on, they ran down on the crusted snow.

The Caldwells told of the thousands of hides that Moodys from The Dalles bought from the bounty hunters before the turn of the century.

Jess Tetherow and his companions got 75¢ for a small hide and $1.50 for a large hide. They stretched them all on wooden frames. For kids, that was good money because hunting was superb in the junipers of Red-mond at the turn of the century. Many of the settlers at Haystack, Opal City, and that sec-tion told of always going to Redmond to get their deer.

Jess used a black powder 44/40 first, graduating to a 32/20 in the smokeless powder transition. He owned a hardwood deer cart, vintage unknown, that hauled out over 200 deer.

Mr. Rogers of the Cove used to freight a wagonload of supplies to the market hunters at Forked Horn Butte, Redmond, where he traded his hams for fresh venison for his family.

Mule deer. (William Van Allen)

Karl Kleinfeldt, with a twinkle in his eye, said of a 40/82 rifle he secured for $10: "I was always thinking seriously of putting a set of Ford wheels under it to move it around easier." For that princely sum, he got with it several pounds of black powder, a loading outfit, bullet mold, and much empty brass.

Grover Caldwell quoted the price of a "thutty-thutty" in 1910 as being $12.50, and shells for it at six-bits a box.

Of the many deer stories, one could have ended differently for the two Weaver brothers who pulled this boner: "We were training a race horse for a Mr. Everly," they said. "We always had jerky hanging around drying, so one day he asked us about making so much, and we told him we bundled it up to sell to Erickson's Saloon in Portland. We heard later he was a game warden."

This inland hunting arena is mule deer country, but Slick Raper told of whitetails they killed on Davis Mountain in earlier years.

As the men I talked to loosed tender-tucked memories of the hunt, the tales fell thick and fast. And being typical hunters,

most were whoppers or about whopper bucks. There were water-stained snapshots to verify some of these narratives. So sit around a make-believe campfire and listen:

There was a deer head mounted in one of the lumber camps that had 21 and 23 points on respective sides.

Dean Harris from Summer Lake told of a nine-point that field-dressed 256 pounds. He added this story: "One year we had a Portlander who came out to these highlands to hunt with us and boasted he would pack out any deer that any of us shot. I got a buck the next day at Bates Butte that dressed out 220 pounds with all the legs cut off at the hocks. He couldn't get it off the ground."

For many seasons, there was a mule deer head with a 43-inch spread hanging over the door of Egglie's station in Silver Lake; today a 30-inch spread is considered a trophy.

The Cal Shermans, from out Crooked River way, had a non-typical head with a total of 32 points gathering dust in one of their sheds for many years. Cal's dad, an inveterate hunter, bagged it.

In 1910, Van Lake killed a granddaddy that

live-dressed 320 pounds. Steve Steidl equals this in telling of one his dad got at Hunter's Butte southeast of Bend that couldn't be balanced with 300-pound weights on his dad's slaughterhouse scales.

Grover Caldwell fondly recalled one monster they got at Brown's Creek on the Upper Deschutes that three grown men couldn't lift to load on their largest horse. They dragged it the short ways to his cabin there. After getting it cut and wrapped, they had 240 pounds of prime venison.

Some seasons, the outdoorsy families of Messingers, Tetherows, and Weavers came back from their trips to Irish and Taylor Lakes with 30 head for their winter's meat. Hides were left on when the weather held cold.

If the deer seem to have a way of confounding the hunter in our time, these pioneer families just sojourned in their tents and dwelt on the mountainsides until all the tags were filled. Living was at a slower pace then.

Venison versus antelope brought varying reactions. The Paul Riedels of Hampstead Valley said antelope were fine eating, but others had reservations. Earl Small, the Silver Lake settler who probably had as much of it for sampling as anyone, said, "They were good until June, but from then on they got strong."

Van Lake was less flattering of the beautiful animals and offered, "They were generally poor eating." On another occasion he observed, "No good in the wintertime."

Some of the trouble in this direction is that no part of the hide should touch the meat during the field dressing and skinning operation. Like a sheep's hide, it imparts a strong muttony taste if one is careless in handling it.

Several ladies among the desert settlers told of the antelope's interesting habit of circling the wash fluttering on the line.

The men had loading sessions during the winter months when there were fewer chores to do. They all saved lead and tin scrap, brought in their loading gear, and met at one of the neighbors. As the hot lead glimmered in the lamplight while the mold got just the right temperature for casting, the silver bullets tumbled out in a steady stream onto soft toweling.

Blue Goose Saloon, Silver Lake, 1912, before it burned down. (Mrs. Thom)

Winter forage for the mule deer. (William Van Allen)

Each bragged of his particular caliber and its virtues. The kids had the messy job of "putting" the grease in the bullet grooves. "Putting" is the word, as there is no neat way of doing it.

Smells permeated the room, of powder, and of the musty odor of horses and livestock clinging to clothes, and of dried manure impressed to boot seams. Soon the whiff of pan-boiled coffee drifted in and the happy chore was done for another few months.

One yarn was told of a camp of hunters tented in the Embody Mill section of the low desert. After three or four days in camp, they had only one spindly flanked, sunken-eyed buck hanging from their meat pole. Two fires and a jug of red-eye weren't doing much to raise their spirits. Supper was over and some luckless party fell victim to the dirty dishes. The rest were rolling smokes or firing up their pipes.

"Hey Johnny, lend me some of your Bull Durham — I'm outa smokes."

No answer.

"Didn'cha hear? How about some tobacco?"

"I got some, but it's pretty high out here. . ."

"Whadda'ya mean, high? Pass it over."

"Well," drawled the other, "what'er ya willin' t'pay?"

"Pay!" he croaked.

Grins that couldn't be hid were blossoming on the bearded faces.

"Guess four bits for makin' a smoke ain't a bad price, is it?"

"Four bits . . !" the other sputtered.

"Ain't no stores out here; tobacco's higher'n hell out this far," said another, blowing tendrils in his direction.

Besides the lousy luck of the hunt, the man settled the issue by paying the extortion demanded of him. Buddies tried and true.

Several wolf stories were told with varying emotions.

Freda McDaniel of Laidlaw told of the time they were running low on firewood and she and her brother, Butch Clark, took the team and wagon and headed west toward Bull Springs for a load. The dog went along, of course. "On the way back," she said, "three gray wolves came cutting across to us and chased the dog right under the wagon. He stayed there every foot of the way home."

She also remembered a day in 1907 when wolves chased a deer through their fields, and again, told of the fate of their neighbor's dog. As was their custom, the neighbors sent the dog after the cattle one evening, but he didn't return; the next day, they found traces of his remains where several wolves had stalked and killed him.

Bill Van Allen said that on their home ranch near Tetherow Butte they saw a wolf. And on a 1910 hunting trip in the Crane Prairie country, his father, uncle, brother, and he saw five in one pack.

More recently, about 1950, Jim Spillane and Leo Herbring rammed their way by Jeep up the Highline Road west of Bend in foothill country. They came upon a freshly killed deer lying in about a foot of snow, looked up, and saw a wolf glowering down at them on a rise. Both of these men are longtime hunters and know a coyote by size from a wolf, but these predators had not been reported in this region for many years, so the men questioned government trappers. The government men volunteered the theory that wolves could have been crossed with police dogs that escaped from Camp Abbot south of Bend on the Deschutes River during the K-9 Corps training days of World War II. When the snows got too deep on the wet western side of the Cascades, the wolves trekked over the lesser snowpack of the east side. Leo said there were prints of several animals around the kill.

Other rare and little-known finds include two buffalo heads and a horn found by the Serman's daughter on the outskirts of their ranch.

Bill Rogers (left) and family. He was a great hunter. "Killed a ibex out of a herd of 13 near Opal City and also a large mountain sheep on the Deschutes River west of Opal City. The skull remained in a juniper tree one third the way down from the top of the rim for many years." Mountain sheep became extinct in Oregon around 1900.

The fate of the desert rams was told in snatches of hunting yarns. One narrator said that in the early days there were "ibex" on crags of Smith Rock, just north of Redmond. Antelope stay on the rolling plains, so he no doubt meant wild sheep.

As late as the days of Bill Brown's riders, one man told of shooting a wild sheep in the remote area between Glass Buttes and Wagontire. The animal was high in the pinnacles. And according to Earl Small, the wild sheep were still in the Summer Lake rims in 1879.

But Grover Caldwell believes the last of the desert rams were killed in the 1890's when the market hunters got them cornered in the broken rims near the head of the Crooked River. "I also found heads at Whitaker Holes, with horns four inches through, full curled, having broomed ends," Grover said, and he had run thousands of domestic sheep in his time, so he knew a wild head.

The elderly Mr. Weaver killed one on top of Bear Creek Butte in 1870. So they disappeared with the passenger pigeon and buffalo.

If the youngsters were constantly exposed to the legendary hunting tales, it is small wonder they were imbued with the intangibles of the chase at an early age.

About Christmas, in 1912, Harry Johnson, Bruce De Armond, Ron Fox, Johnny Bates, Cal Hunter, and Ivan McGillvray of Bend gathered their arsenal for a long-planned trip upriver on the Big Deschutes.

"We were going to stay at Minear's cabin on the river," Mr. McGillvray said, "but we had a long, cold ride by stage to the town of Lava. We got dumped off there, and had to cut west across country over two feet of snow to search for the cabin. It was hard going, and we were wet, cold, and miserable as it started getting dark. One of the boys lost his dad's revolver. We finally found the cabin and all crowded in. We couldn't find a candle or get a lantern lit for awhile, so we started smashing boards to make kindling for a fire. We made kindling all right! In the confusion, we broke up a brand new shotgun, still crated, that one of us had brought along for the hunt. Three of the kids talked all night long and kept the rest of us awake. I guess we were all scared. But we came back with some ducks, and luckily, came back in spring and found the lost revolver. But that shotgun was a pitiful sight, and ruined."

Do the inland expanses of Oregon have rattlesnakes? Yes and no. For vast stretches of sagelands, the answer is no, and for miles of the Cascade foothills and mountains there are none. But in scattered areas of the desert and in many of the river canyons lying north, there are some. Powell Butte, Bear Creek Butte, and Glass Buttes house the venomous critters.

In the main, there seems to be something about the pumice sand abounding here that rattlers don't like. Also it is cold in these rangelands, frosting every month in the summer most years. Yet the fishermen, rockhounds, and arrowhead hunters should watch closely in their wanderings. Gladys Meeks Workman, whose folks ran Halfway House at Hampton, remembers more than one school outing or 4th of July picnic that was run out of the Glass Buttes and Stauffer

Freight team pulling into Brookings Half-Way House on Bend-Burns Highway. (Brookings photo)

areas because of snakes.

J. R. Roberts, of Redmond, told of a trip he took with R. H. Bailey to Grandview to see a large blasting job in 1909. "He saw a rattler," Mr. Roberts said, "and took a juniper limb and pinned its head down. While I held it, he took a grass straw and cleaned his pipe stem, then drew it through the snake's mouth. It was dead in less than a minute from the nicotine."

According to one settler, there was a little island of high ground between the Harmon Ranch and Halfway House, north of the Burns highway, "that had plenty of them." "We always stayed away from there!" he added. And typical of their spotty population is the fact that this man lived three miles from this spot and saw only one on his home ranch in 40 years.

A bachelor ranching at Pancake Hill of Powell Butte slept in an alcove he had built fronting his house to the east and west. It insured cool sleeping during hot summer spells. Stairs entered it from each end. One night, as he pulled off his shoes making ready for bed, his dog started raising a terrific commotion at something under the cot. The man went to the kitchen and got a kerosene lamp, then pulled the bed away from the wall to investigate. Coiled up a mere 18 inches from his pillow end of his bed, the snake lay snuggled on the porch floor. The faithful dog sniffed out the stair-climbing snake.

Of cougars, there were also tales told.

Marie Brosterhous and other girls of her school class mentioned the two large cats the menfolks got west of Bend in 1904. When she and her friends were going down the boardwalk on their way home, a small knot of people were crowded around the two pumas. It was no trick for the girls to squeeze through the ring of humanity, but they were mighty impressed at the seemingly immense length of those mature animals.

Several others told of hearing the cougars scream at night. Most knew a coyote's call, some knew an owl's call, so it probably wasn't that. Self-professed experts say a cougar won't scream. Whatever it was the people heard was real and impressive.

Mrs. Pittman Stout related the time she had a small band of youngsters on a walk to the Little Deschutes, close by Rosland. Stretched out, sleeping in a small patch of sunlight lay a cougar. The chaperone restrained the kids with outstretched arms, but the sudden quiet awakened the cat. A tense few seconds followed as it lay with its head to the ground, ears flattened, tail twitching. For a short eternity, the feline's eyes bored into the group, then it sprang into the air and was out of sight in three or four leaps. The walk was over.

Mrs. Stout also told of her frustrated attempts to raise chickens while living at La Pine. The eagles and hawks kept them thinned out until her husband put small saplings across the pens in a primitive roof. It worked only until the predators learned to dive-bomb between them. Meanwhile, the infantry was at work along with the Air Force. The chipmunks had a cute trick. They hopped into the nests and flipped the eggs onto the floor, then rolled them out any opening they could find. Finally, in desperation, the Stouts stretched chicken wire over the saplings. Egg production picked up considerably after that. The bird predators broke their necks in diving until they, too, were thinned out.

A shepherd used to cross Clark's place each spring and fall while taking his band of woolies through the Laidlaw settlement to and from the mountains. Each season, he stayed for a good home-cooked meal or two

while his pack string fed in their pasture. One night, a cougar stampeded the horses through a barbed wire fence. One mount was badly cut and the other was not found till the next spring. For a time after that, the Clark's cows were bothered so badly at night that they would tear down the corrals and run for miles. None of the settlers were able to trap or shoot the culprit.

As late as the 1950's, a puma made his hunting circle to include the water tanks on Overturf Butte, at Bend's west city limits. His tracks were seen and indentified in the snow.

More rare than cougars was another livestock killer named "Old Yank" of the Yamsey Mountain area. The demise of this bear was noteworthy enough that it made the San Francisco papers.

In 1899, George Small and Jeff Howard took his track after he had killed a three-year-old out of a bunch of cattle that Mr. Small and young Earl were riding herd on.

"We raised steers to four years old then, but Old Yank had been partial to the younger steers, and had taken his toll from many ranchers," Earl said. "The elderly Mr. Vandevert had hounds and told us to let him know when the bear struck again."

They were driving some steers to Klamath Marsh and had passed through Buck Creek on the Coshow Place when the bruin got another. They dispatched a letter to Mr. Vandevert, but the mail took a week by stage, so before the hounds arrived a few men got together and started tracking. The bear went so high in the snows, however, that the men gave up for a time.

Earl continued: "Creed Conn, Mr. Vandevert, Jeff Howard, my dad, and several others I can't remember now started after him again. I was 12 at the time but begged my dad until he gave in and let me tag along.

"Bill Ball, who was part Indian, had heard the men talking of the last cattle kills while at the hotel in town, and took off and hit our camp late that night. He got up early and stole off while the rest still slept. The men found the bear tracking a deer, but also found Ball's track on theirs, too. They heard shooting far above them.

"We all hurried forward and found the

Brookings Half-Way House
Second from left is Horace Brookings. (Evelyn Brookings)

Indian on a high rock in front of a den. We had two shepherd dogs with us; one ran, but the other stayed.

"My dad gave me a .44 revolver, put me up on a rock, and told me to stay put. Then the men gathered stuff for a smudge to smoke the animal out. All this took time and it was getting along toward evening when someone cut a long pole. With the men standing by with guns, another poked through the opening to provoke him into a charge. He came at the men with a rush, but the small hole slowed him down at the entrance. The half-breed shot him.

"The next day, we skinned him. Mother got several cans of bear grease for hair, boots, and chest colds. Later, I got up at the Literary Society and told my story, but no one believed me until I showed them some of the claws I had. I sold one to a fellow for 50¢, I remember. We got $2.50 for the hide, which measured nine feet long. His foot was 18'' x 12'','' said Earl.

The Lava Bears. Where did the name come from? How many settlers had ever seen one? Are they still here or are they fictitious?

The first account given by an old-timer was told by P. B. Johnson, who ran the Millican store for years. "A small brown bear was shot on the desert on our south boundary in August of 1916 or 1917," he said. "The hide was nailed on Gilmore's homestead shack, and was there for many years."

This item was filed in a horde of other notes, then forgotten. But a tip from someone that Marjorie Smith of Bend had many old snapshots and papers of the Farewell Bend days led to pay dirt. In *The Western Tourist* of October 1910 was found the following:

Central Oregon, and the Bend country, especially between Bend and Lakeview, is distinguished by having a species of bear the like of which is not found elsewhere in so far as it is able for us to ascertain.

This little bear is called by the stockmen, the Lava Bear, and as its name implies, is found in the vast stretches of impenetrable lava in northern Lake County. The little animal is very rare and stockmen who have spent their lifetime in the Silver Lake valley have seen but a very few of them. One of these men who has ridden the range for thirty years has, in that time, seen only four specimens of this rare animal. On one or two occasions individual animals have been taken in traps by coyote hungers, and it was in this manner that the Biological Survey became interested in learning more of this strange species, ranging from two to three feet in length and eighteen to twenty-four inches in height.

A prominent Klamath Falls sheepman also sent one of these dwarfed specimens to The Dalles, where it was mounted and on exhibit for some time. They are peculiarly built, and appear to be rather bunched up or dwarfed. In color they range from mixed brown to a decided cinnamon, although nearly all specimens have a somewhat grizzled appearance.

In examining the anatomy of the bears, particularly the skulls, the Biological Survey, through its naturalists, as well as other eminent scientists, have pronounced it as true grizzly, as differentiated from the ordinary black bear. In other words, it is a dwarfed species of grizzly similar to the dwarfed mountain sheep found in the mountains of the state of Chihuahua, Mexico.[4]

Then Irving S. Cobb entered the picture. He was in this country on an extended hunting trip and, upon hearing of this little-known bruin, was determined to capture or shoot one:

From Crater Lake the drive was made to Fort Rock in one day. Here they were joined by A. Andrews, the trapper of that section for the U. S. Biological Survey, and a trip was made into the lava fields northwest of Fort Rock (Devils Garden) to look at the home of the small bear which inhabits that section, in the vain hope of finding one of them out on the edge of the lava.

Water was taken on at Edward's ranch, and a two days' trip made to the fields, but without success, except to find a number of tracks several weeks old. Mr. Cobb was intensely interested in the stories of this rare bear, as told by the men who have seen them, and by the still fewer number who have killed one.

That these lava fields are the home of the "Sun" bear, which has been supposed to be an extinct species for the past fifteen years, is the firm conviction of Mr. Cobb, and he has made arrangements with trapper Andrews to take one of the animals alive next year when the question will be determined.

The bear is known locally by several names, the most common being the lava bear. It is also called locally, sand lapper, and dwarf grizzly, resembling the big grizzly in shape and color to a great extent.[5]

After this windfall of information, some backtracking to former Silver Lake and Fort Rock residents was necessary. It paid off.

One veteran of that era told me that Mr. Andrews, the government trapper, did indeed trap one of these uncommon bears. Another animal got into a lava crevice, but it was injured in getting taken out and later died. The live specimen was exhibited around the various towns and settlements for well over a year. No one recalled the fate of that little sun bear. Had it been well known how few of them remained, the government officials might have been able to save the species.

Earl Small added, "One was trapped alive on Uncle Jim's ranch. We had that one just a few days and it disappeared."

Another settler, long in that country, told of the government man who trapped two and toured the whole state with the live one of the

[4] R. A. Ward, *The Western Tourist,* October, 1920, vol. I, no. 1, pg. 6.
[5] Ibid., p. 27.

pair surviving for two years or more.

It is apparent from all the overlapping information that the last known survivor of this kind disappeared about 1920.

I am a hunter and have handled guns since before my teens. Many lives have been stilled by my weapons, without thought, without a nagging conscience. The chipmunks and rock chucks were not killed for food. Neither were the bobcats and coyotes killed to protect my flocks, because I had none to protect.

Why then did I kill? Why do others of my kind continue to do so? It is a question we should ask ourselves, and if we do, the answer comes home to roost: We are predators, the most destructive predators God has put on earth.

I camp much alone. Now I save the small woodsfolk to keep me company. My rifle will never be raised against a coyote again. Because somewhere along that trail of carcasses the message will sink in.

It can come in a sudden unforgettable moment when our baser thoughts have transcended into a realization that wilderness is necessary to our being, that these wild creatures are as much a part of this fleeting existence here as we are. As more of this permeates our being, we note trifling incidents and dramas in nature we have been missing for years.

On occasion, the hard-bitten hunters also showed a sentimental side. The hunt wasn't all killing.

An old-timer was gassing with an assortment of elk hunters in the Strawberry Mountain vicinity and told wistfully of his first buck: "I was so little that it took both hands to hold the .45 revolver when the old folks put me on stand. To steady myself, I put my arms on a stump as tall as I was. I suddenly heard the hollow boom of an approaching deer. I fired, and after the terrific roar, walked over to my first buck."

This man died in an elk camp, where he would have wanted to die. He asked to have his ashes spread on the spot where, so many years ago in the cold morning hours, he had shot his first deer. So it was done. A low-flying plane dipped a wing as a hunter's ashes fluttered down on his ridge of many hunts.

Of the rich array of animals the west has housed in past centuries, several have vanished from this land, their home. As the last echoes of a shot pulsed its way across the barren lava land, a species had been lost. The buffalo, the desert ram, the giant grizzly, the miniature lava bear, and the wolf all once knew this earth and called it home. Then with the coming of the settlers, the cutting of the forests, the stringing of wire, and the entrance of the Durhams and the sheep, the relentless press against their rims and crags and remoteness began.

Among the old-timers, some talked wistfully of the early hunting. Others said they had put up their rifles and scatter-guns on the mantel to gather dust. Yet some active nimrods in their seventies and eighties still look forward with enthusiasm to going afield each fall.

Yet most, in their sometimes rough and unlettered talk, were philosophical. The gist of what they endeavored to say is that first they were killers and last they became sportsmen.

They all told tricks of the trade they used. One said, "We stripped pine needles off in a tub and layered our clothes in them for a day or two before a hunt." Another, from La Pine, was remembered and talked about for a peculiar habit he had. Every little while in his stalking, he would place a damp cloth thinly over his nose to help him to "smell" any deer about.

Yet I know many hunters who can smell both deer and elk, especially in a much used area. Not too many generations back, in Miles Standish times, there is documented evidence that the Indians of that day recognized each other in the dark by their individual smells.

One particularly successful hunter saved the scent glands that had been cut off the deer legs the previous year. When ready to use, they were soaked to activate the scent and rubbed into his pants.

Today, the legendary hunting grounds are still waiting. Steller's Marsh, Lookout Mountain, Three-Fingered Jack to the south and west, Grizzly and Ashwood to the north, Hampton Butte and the broken lava rims to the east, hemlock, spruce, cutover, sageland — the choice is yours.

When we are touched by the magic of the hunt, each trip becomes an enchanted reality. We head for the wild uncertainty of a favorite haunt, leaving behind the cluttered debris of civilization. Storm clouds are a veiled warning of a tempest to come, but for now, we will be steeped in the silence of the land and will cherish it.

And if we heed the sentiments voiced by Justice Bok, many years ago, that "The truly gifted soul lives in an attitude of courtesy to the universe," the land will be ours to cherish for many generations to come.

CHAPTER 19

The People

Excerpts from some of the pioneer books and newspapers are too colorful to pass up. An article from the Prineville *News* of June 1887 by George Barnes contained the following:

We had to cross over snow twenty feet deep, but we arrived at Camp Polk without any mishaps and found Captain White in good spirits and the cattle safe.

The following day we loaded up and started for Ochoco, arriving at Wayne Claypool's in two and half days. This was, certainly, as fine a country then as a stock man could wish to see. The bottoms were covered with wild rye, clover, pea vines, wild flax and meadow grass that was waist high on horseback. The hills were clothed with a mat of bunch grass that seemed inexhaustible. . . . Johnson and I went to hauling rails, and I have always believed that if untoward events and the Indians had not interfered I would have reached the top round of the ladder of fame as a bull whacker. For even now I look back with feelings of pride and longing regret to those bright sunny mornings when we arose with the lark and sage tick and joyously ambled down to the spring branch, bathed our expansive brows, scoured our pitch-covered hands and with appetites that passed all understanding, did ample justice to the ability of our cook, and blythly took our way to the rail patch with an ox gad in one hand, a trusty United States gun on one shoulder, and two Colt's revolvers swung to our belts, and let our fine soprano voices ring out on the morning air. [1]

***Prineville Bank.** (McCoin photo)*

***Prineville street scene: Smith & Clerk, Reception, Rideout & Foster, the general furnishing store, and Prineville Bank.** (McCoin photo)*

[1] In *An Illustrated History of Central Oregon*, p. 704.

Looking east over Prineville, 1913. (Roberts photo)

Also, from a similar source dated 1870 there was a mixture of humor and history concerning Prineville's start:

During that summer (1868) Barney Prine started Prineville by building a dwelling house, store, blacksmith shop, hotel and saloon. I think he was all of one day building them. They were constructed of willow logs, 10 by 14 in size, one story high and all under one roof. His first invoice of goods cost $80; his liquor consisted of a case of Hostetter's Bitters (about 40 percent alcohol), and the iron for the blacksmith shop was obtained from the fragments of an old emigrant wagon left up on Crooked River. In addition to his other business ventures, Barney laid out and made a race track that ran from the banks of Crooked River up along where now is the north side of First Street, and many were the bottles of Hostetter's lost and won over that track by the local racers of the period. Right here I want to tell of the first poker game played in this country which was also my first venture in that direction.

A few days before the game some one from The Dalles had brought out a wagon-load of apples which Barney had purchased. On this day I happened to go to the "town" and

Barney took me out and very solicitously inquired if I was versed in the mysteries of "draw," stating that if I would go in with him we could make a "raise" out of some Warm Spring Indians who were camped on the river and wanted a game. I very frankly confessed my almost criminal ignorance in that useful branch of a boy's education; that my parents had not been able to send me to college, so my education was limited to a country school grade; but I was willing to learn; as he told me that if I would sit just to his right and "cut" the cards just to his "break" we would go through those Indians like a case of the itch in a country school. I consented and we soon had the game in full blast; Barney and I and two of the Indians. Barney would run up hands and I would "cut," generally using both hands to get the "cut" correct. My work was a little "coarse" but I got there "Eli" all the same. Those Indians could speak only two English words, "I passe," and every time Barney and I would get in a good shuffle and "cut" those confounded heathens would ejaculate "I passe," with an unanimity that was paralyzing to our hope as it was astonishing, and when it came their turn to deal, the surprising hands that would be out! But the most singular part of it all was, invariably one of the condemned Indians would have the top hand, and it was not long before the Indians had all of Barney's money, and I am inclined to believe that it was all the money in the settlement at that time. After our money had all been lost we bet apples at $4 a box, and it was not long before the Indians had won the entire load of apples. Then the game stopped. We were busted. We had nothing else the Indians wanted. I stood and watched them load their ponies with the apples and when they started off I turned to my partner and whispered, "Barney, I pass." He just snorted and said that any one was a blanked fool to play with a blankety blank "Stolen Bottle," though what resemblance there was between those Indians and a stolen bottle I couldn't perceive.[2]

An amateur historian can readily see that our dates in western history come late. Many wouldn't consider these latecomers pioneers, but they traveled by horsepower, slept in ash and oak wagons or rag houses, kept the wrinkles out of their bellies with sage hens, antelope, and mule deer. They drank right from the creeks and rivers or dipped it out of a wooden barrel.

Two companies that were doing a bang-up job of enticing newcomers from as far east as Tennessee and the Carolinas were the D.I.P. Company (Deschutes Irrigation and Power) and Poor and Poor.

So the people came. They left the monumental trappings of civilization to come. They left fine and affluent families to wage quiet and relentless war with a harsh desert or primitive forest. There were no fife and

---

[2] Ibid., pp. 723-724.

Gas lights and city hall on Wall Street, Bend, 1910. (John Munion photo)

Wastina School and class (near Fort Rock and now a ghost town). Early '30s. (Walters photo)

drums to greet them in this new land. They were students-in-residence learning the manifest difficulties of stringing a tight fence and skinning and gutting a mule deer. Primitive skills, once known to their grandparents, were relearned by word of mouth at basket socials, dances, and country gatherings. And if the skills were not learned here, the painful method of trial and error was even more indelible. Castrating an animal or single-jacking a well through lava layers replaced punching a time clock or catching a 7 o'clock trolley in Saint Joe or Saint Paul. And the newcomers' teething rings in this rebirth included bucking and splitting juniper logs or sticking a bloated steer between the proper ribs to save it.

A shortage of money settled the issue of returning for some; they were broke, so they stayed and got work. In a few years, they bore the stamp of the desert and stayed long enough to kick dust in the faces of the next generations while being raised on a diet of frost, juniper, lava rock, and sage.

Around the new hamlets, jobs were plentiful. A rotund Dale Tusing told me of his first day in Bend. In walking four blocks, he was offered four jobs. But he was headed for Burns by horseback. A webfoot, he had always wanted to see the desert, so he headed out into its peculiar desolation, camping on the way. It was awash with spring blooms, and a quiet abounded that fascinated him. He took water where he could for his mount, paying many different prices for the liquid.

The promise of wealth from wheat, timber claims, or even gold pulled pilgrims to a land of cowboys who seldom bathed. Yet there was another lure, one that would not be denied. It was for exploration — a lure deeply basic in the human spirit — that they moved. The settlers were human thistledown drifting to the yellow pine and the sagelands.

The newcomers planted, but the forests devoured the fruits of the soil. The silent desert watched their futile attempts with serene indifference. Wheat was quickly replaced by rye, oats, and barley; tomato sets and cucs were replaced by root crops. As Jack Eby quipped every spring, "They're going to be caught with their plants down!"

The land locaters used to "salt" squash, onions, and so forth in abandoned cellars they conveniently happened to pass when leading homesteaders to their newly acquired land. A few "crop leftovers" lying carelessly about often clinched a deal where a lack of words became a wise discretion.

These were the thin years, getting started.

Anyone having a way with horses worked in liveries, drove stage or freight teams, or rode for wild horses, a transient crop the high desert furnished. In a few years, the settlers' bottom halves betrayed their riding habits and their faces were lined from being fired in the kiln of the desert. They spent twice as much time in the saddle as in a bedroll for the better part of their lives, learning this was cattle and horse country instead of the fine farm land they had envisioned.

As the desert dropouts multiplied, the remainders soon jailed the land into little kingdoms with barbed wire. And they asked questions: "How big should the shack be?" "Where can we get the lumber?" "How far to the nearest water?" "Should we get a milk cow?"

The location settled many of these issues. The sagebrush homesteads were far removed from lumber and timber sources. Near Grizzly Mountain, Mailings, Durhams, and Pecks did a flourishing trade. Steidls set up their mill in Bend in 1902. Elid Ammon ran the Maury Mountain mill. Embody Mill, near the ghost town of Wastina in the Fort Rock sector, built that area up in gleaming shacks. That spot is still listed on maps the deer hunters use as a landmark.

Steve Steidl recalled his dad's daily cut was 40,000 feet a day. Steve, a tall, spare man, could spin many a tale of those early days.

Lumber was $8 to $10 a thousand in 1911, not a bad price by today's standard, but those were one-hundred-cent dollars in that period. At a-dollar-a-day wages, most ate hard-earned bread. So they built small.

When winter swept across the high plateau and the wind had venom in its lips, the settlers were glad they had built small. Every foot of space had to be heated. Cordwood sold for $2, come and get it, or $3 delivered, near the towns. But most people trundled out into the hinterlands and worked their own up, by crosscut, wagon and team.

Those who a few years back didn't know tamarack from tamarisk learned what woods were best for heating. In the sagelands, juniper was the standby, but if that tree had a thousand years of time wrapped up in that tattered bark, it still had its drawbacks. The bark was blown full of sand from centuries of desert storms, the trunks were inevitably hollow, and the incredibly tough limbs were just plain hell on clothes and saw teeth. But it made a wonderful wood with a smoke that, once smelled, was not soon forgotten.

John Steidl had the first bank in Bend. (Steve Steidl photo)

JOHN STEIDL, PRESIDENT

Central Oregon Banking & Trust Company

Capital $25,000

BEND, OR.

ON ACCOUNT OF THE HEAVY WITHDRAWELS MADE ON US DURING THE PAST SIX OR SEVEN WEEKS, THIS BANK WILL BE CLOSED FOR A FEW DAYS OR UNTIL WE CAN REALIZE ON OUR COLLECTIONS AND SECURITIES.

DEC. 17th. 1907. Central Oregon Banking & Trust Co.

On the sandflats and in the foothills, jack pine became a favorite. Some called it lodgepine, *Pinus contorta*, but books list jack pine as a separate species, *Pinus banksiana*. Whatever the name, the trees were easily worked up. The limbs popped off with a healthy whack and the wood burned clean, leaving less ash than juniper. Cut green in the spring, jack pine could be halved, summered in ricks, and by October it was prime fuel.

In the big timber, dead, blue-skinned ponderosas were the object of the annual wood haul. In the Sister-Camp Polk area, red fir or tamarack lined the lean-to wood sheds.

But probably the easiest source of wood was to follow the logging operations and gather up the broken up yellow pine limbs. They were abundant and they took little work. They were brittle-hard and somewhat pitchy. But this latter fact was undoubtedly the primary cause of the numerous fires plaguing all the hamlets in yellow pine country. Soot and carbon slowly built up from these rich chunks of fuel until a roaring chimney fire overheated a flimsy metal pipe and another conflagration resulted.

Scenes of pastoral simplicity depicting the kitchen range as the centerpiece could have been painted in the period from October to April. Popcorn popped joyously and the teakettle sang lustily while lamps anointed the room with a soft halo of light — this was the typical family scene.

Many a young housewife was surprised to learn that her chickens were bait for hawks and coyotes. A .22 rifle became as much a part of her wares as an eggbeater. There were other sometimes strange or difficult things for these young mothers to adjust to. Most got a shock at their first sight of the homestead shack; years later, several admitted to tears of disappointment at that introduction. Not only the distaff side was thus affected but the men as well found it difficult to adapt to a new environment. One lady in recounting those harsh times said simply, "The desert killed my husband. The discouragement, the disappointments killed him."

Some with a little bankroll outlasted their neighbors, but unless their crops rustled in luxury for several years running, they too headed for town for a steady and less worrisome income.

Those that stayed took a slab of land and partly civilized it. But some of that land's primitive juices drained into them, too. Even those that left, whether reluctantly or willingly, made an annual pilgrimage back, years after they had left their plot. Was it to hear the heartbeat of a world that lay high, and still, and dry? And what were the memories that washed over them in gentle waves as they stood where a sun-bleached board bellied to the sun among bits of purpling glass? In the sand flat, they saw the dabbled print of a coyote — who still owned the land.

Their memories were simple and their glory scanty. They were not brushed by immortality, and what glory they had now lies in the dust of a pioneer grave.

Adulthood came early for these early settlers. Time and again, ages of 10 and 12 were given as the years that people took to riding herds, cutting wood, planting, harvesting, skinning, gutting, and branding.

Typical of this was a tale Dean Harris told, while retired in Bend: "When I was a kid, I liked to read. If we didn't have too much schooling, we read every chance we got. We had a drive of cattle going in the Summer Lake district. It was winter, and the cattle balked at crossing an icy stream. For a long time, the men cursed while their mounts milled around trying to get the cattle to brave that frigid water. I finally roped a calf and dragged it across to the other side where it stood bawling for its ma. In just a few seconds, she splashed across to that little bugger to see if it was alright. The rest followed, and the drive was on."

Dean was just a kid of 11 or so, but he had read about that trick in a western magazine.

Other tales were told with tongue in cheek.

"A couple of sprouts had a pet rooster," someone said, "a smart one because it could crow in two languages. One day a huge dust devil came swirling by, making a mess of things. When the cleanup was over, someone noticed the rooster was gone. A couple of

Stagecoach at historic trail crossing of Crooked River Gorge, a mile or so east of present bridge on U.S. Highway 97. Roberts of Redmond sign is still visible on the cliff. 1910. (Slack photo)

The Redmond Stage crossing the Crooked River, 1910. (Mrs. Thom)

Clark Green Rogers, the man who homesteaded the famous "Cove" on the Crooked River. His fruit was delivered all over the area. (McCoin photo)

days passed before one of the kids heard it crowing way out in the rabbit brush. And he was mad. (They always suspected it had fighting cock in it.) It was blowed into a small-necked gallon jug and it was naked as a jaybird. They had to break the jug to get him out," the straight-faced narrator concluded.

The steady trickle of homesteaders came, paying $1.25 an acre in timber or sageland, with 14 months to pay for their plot. Taxes ran around $10 at first, and later $18 a section.

The canyon country north of Bend and Redmond had its share of settlers. So it was that in 1878 the Osborne family let their logs down by rope over the east wall of the Crooked River Canyon, where theirs became one of the first homes in the bunchgrass-covered country. This spot, a veritable Garden of Eden, was later famed throughout the Pacific Northwest as Cove State Park. For years, it was near the top in attendance of picnickers among Oregon's parks. Enticing the visitors were about 300 fruit trees the pioneer family had planted and replanted as disease and age took tool of their stock. An itinerant wagoner, leather-faced Alkali Ike, made trips each August and September from the canyon bottom to distribute the fresh bounty of apricots, apples, peaches, and plums to the outlying populace as long as it would last. Now that original homestead, so rich in the area's lore, lies drowned under some 200 feet of backwater from one of the two dams Portland General Electric put in for power.

Among crops the Osborne and Rogers clans had to keep in check were rattlesnakes and the head-high wild ryegrass.

"Later, the men made a boat so we could cross the river to hunt mule deer and fish," Mrs. Osborne's fascinating family diary told. Her husband recounted one of his dad's hunting tales when a party of four climbed to "No Man's Land," as they called the Peninsula. A mule deer buck was shot and wounded and half-fell, half-leaped over the awesome crags to a small ledge several feet below. Four other deer followed, but the ledge was too small to hold them, and all five plunged the more than 400 feet to the bottom. It took the men more than an hour to reach them but, upon examining them, they found the animals too broken to use.

"That same day my dad killed what may have been one of the last of the desert rams," George said. "Thirty-three years later, the head of that ram was found by a party of railroad survey crews scouting the top of that plateau. The railroad crew brought it to a store in the booming town of Metolious, where it was exhibited."

There were many other families colonizing the various sections of this new land. The Vandeverts settled in the 1880's in Powell Butte. The Zumwalts were heading towards Sisters with a $65 stake to carry them through that first winter. The Ketchums landed in Prineville in 1878, the Windoms, Reads, and McCoins at Haystack in the middle 1880's. The Haystack post office was in business in 1882. The immigrant Tetherows settled on the Deschutes north of Redmond in 1887. The Weavers, whose father was born on an immigrant train in 1858, landed on the lower Crooked River in the middle eighties. Later the McCall family took over their holdings.

When Mr. Weaver splurged on a brand new wood range for his wife, she wasn't too happy. She had cooked in cast-iron kettles

Vandeverts and neighbors getting winter's meat at Powell Butte in 1880's.

Vandevert homestead in 1880's on north side of Powell Butte.

July 4th, 1910 on Wall Street, Bend. (Francis Roberts photo)

over a fireplace for so many years that she burned her biscuits and cakes for several weeks afterward on the new stove. Both Lonnie and Charlie, who lived in Bend, were related to Jess Tetherow, a Redmond pioneer. The boys' dad bagged one of the last of the rare desert rams in the hills near Bear Creek, east of Bend.

Other early settlers were the Moffits in the Powell Butte area, the Caldwells of Paulina Prairie, and Earl Small's dad who bought land in the low desert of Silver Lake in 1879.

The dates were late, but millions of logs of virgin ponderosa had yet to feel their pitch blood flow, the rivers to yield their daily limit of 125 fish a day, the buttes to host hunters seeking their four bucks a season. The sheep and wild horse and cattle barons had their empires yet to build.

All this was untapped, and the Johnny-come-lately pioneers were busting to do it.

It would be both silly and false to deny that these settlers lived off the land and the game thereon.

A sprightly Mrs. Zumwalt of Sisters told how they met two trappers at Cold Springs on the way to that hamlet that first winter.

"They gave us their cabin with a dirt floor, bunks, and a large cast-iron cooking kettle for the fireplace," she said. "My brother was a good hunter. We cut a supply of wood and made hay before the snows came, and another went to the valley for beans and flour. With the venison we got, we ate well all winter."

Again, Dean Hollinshead recounts a time when he was just a sprout that several of the families in the La Pine area needed meat: "One morning we were all in the sitting room and dad jumped up and grabbed his 40/65 rifle and got six deer with five shots. What we didn't use, we gave to our neighbors."

The hides were dried and stacked until the Indians came through to trade for them. Of the deer, they made mince meat and jerky and smoked hams. The 1858 Ball fruit jars held many a delicious quart of venison. Indeed, this hunting bit was so indelible in some minds it was recorded on tombstones at death.

The stalwarts ranging into the country south of here, originally with the ill-fated Donner party, split up with them and headed north. The Rev. J. A. Cornwall and family built the first immigrant cabin in Douglas County near Cabin Creek. A plaque dedicated

Bond Street, Bend, in 1914 or 1915 had an abundance of saloons.

to this event reads: "The family wintered here in 1846, 1847. Were saved from extreme want by Israel Stoley, a nephew, who was a good hunter."

Killer winters recorded by word and mouth were the years 1874-75, 1879-80, 1880-81, 1889-90, and 1893. Marsh Awbrey lost most of his cattle the first three winters of the eighties. And others listed *An Illustrated History of Central Oregon* forfeited half to 90 percent of their animals to the bitter elements.

The Osbornes had 1,400 head at the east end of Juniper Butte when the storm of '84 hit. Two of their men stayed with the live-stock and cut juniper trees and dragged them around and around by horse through the chemise brush to expose the tops for feed, but the storm persisted until many of the animals smothered from the driving snow. The sheep were especially hard hit, but so were the cattle from their habit of heading or traveling into the teeth of a storm.

After the weather cleared, one hired man went up on Haystack Butte to skin the dead animals for hides. "He broke one ski on the way down and slid the long slope on a large

hide to reach the ranch buildings," Mrs. Osborne said.

Two of the Osbornes' neighbors for the first few years were H. C. Belknap and Thomas Jenkins, coming in 1876 and 1878, from the Willamette side of the Cascades.

Trips coming east, over the primitive McKenzie Pass and its harsh lava flow, took a terrible toll on cattle and horses. Exhaustion, lack of food, and cripples from the unholy outcroppings left many weak ones behind. Both this pass and Seven Mile Hill on the Santiam claimed their share of victims, and bones marked these trails for years.

Of their trip, one pioneer lady wrote: "During the night, the horses wandered off, hobbles and all, and took off for Webfoot."

It was a hard-and-fast rule on the tough mountain passes that kids walked. The small wagons were taken apart and lifted on to the banks so the larger ones could pass by.

Many did as the Windoms did when they came and packed their dishes in barrels of grain on that first trip, cooked some of the grain during the winter, and planted what was left in the spring.

The newcomers that ended their travels in

the more well-known Sisters, Bend, La Pine, Redmond, or Haystack had no difficulty in locating on land. But as they moved farther east past Millican to Brothers, Hampstead Valley, and Glass Buttes, many could not find their plots when they headed back with a wagonload of supplies and possessions.

Several of the early locals who had farming in mind passed up fortunes in timber claims. Claude Vandevert said, "We passed up huge stands of yellow pine to settle on the more open jack pine and bitterbrush lands we needed for cattle feed." Claude still lived at his homestead property, a lovely spot on the Little Deschutes a few miles north of La Pine.

In those days, the ponderosa stands were so virgin and primitive that no sunlight could come through to aid in the growth of under-brush. From southeast to southwest of Bend, that virgin timber colonnaded the slopes and flats in great, deep green waves.

As the settlers got into a routine and found leisure time, they explored the forests, the sagelands, the lava flows, and the Cascades. In the malipai, the caves and fissures and air holes intrigued them. Seldom were they found in the conventional manner of caves against a sidehill. More often they were circular openings hidden in the flat desert floor by sage and rabbit brush.

The ice caves caught the settlers' fancy. Picnics were eagerly planned, the custard mixed at home then brought along to put in the hand-crank freezer when the party reached the ice cave. Slabs and chips were brought out from the cool recesses of the caves, and the kids took their turns, with varying degrees of willingness, fighting for the clapper.

On these and other trips, the men brought back axed-off pieces and buried them in juniper needles (sawdust was used later). Many of Bend's early homes had this primitive insulation poured into the walls. A tub or two could be gotten from under each large juniper.

The bunchgrass and sagelands got old and monotonous after months on end, so a piney woods outing was at least an annual affair. The families got together during the huckle-

Traveling Dentist

Dr. Harold Clark, Bend's first dentist, with Mrs. Clark in buggy. Some pioneers still carry his work with them. (McCoin photo)

berry season, loaded quilts, tents, buckets, grub, and rifles to head for Roaring Springs, Tombstone Flat, or High Rock for a two or three week trip.

Jess Tetherow and the Weaver boys fondly remembered these trips. The early morning hours were spent in deer hunting. Then came a huge breakfast. Berries were picked until sometime after noon, when they were kept in the deep shade. About four, the men quit again to hunt until dark.

"When the Indians had good luck hunting, they brought over a slab or two of flanks, or a quarter," Lonnie Weaver recalled. "If we had first luck, we did the same. On these trips, the kids all rode horseback; the folks rode the wagons," he added.

The stripling towns were all free-swinging settlements. Bend housed 12 saloons in 1910 when Jack Arnold took the census of its 300 people. But as the rails were threading their steel skeins from the north, any tent cities bordering these operations were still less tamed.

Mrs. Henderson recalled her parents' admonition about "us kids not leaving the homestead and going near Metolius or Culver" when the track crews were in that section.

The gallon houses did a bustling business, and many an impromptu race or wrestling match was talked up over a round or two of drinks. One such took place at the north end of Bend's Wall Street near the Pilot Butte Inn. Bill Pyatt, a small Irishman, had a half-Arabian horse that didn't look like much but ran like the wind. In the course of events, a challenge was flung at him by a fellow member of the Wall Street Potable & Drinking Society. They all streamed out into the street, leaving the bar stools and spitoons behind them. The course was measured, bets were placed all around, and the race was on.

As Bill's mount drew abreast of the other horse to pass him, the rider struck Bill's mount in the face with a riding whip and, of course, Bill lost.

"That made me mad," Bill said with a feather of Irish brogue, "and I told him I could beat his dom horse afoot! I was pretty fleet in those days."

This was too good to keep, and the word was swiftly passed around so more bets could be placed on the match.

The course was shortened a little. Someone fired the starting shot. Bill was off in a leap that caught the horse standing. With feet fairly flying, he sped toward the stake, cut on a dime, and gave his bettors eight cents change. The horse sloughed far around, and Bill dug in to the slight uphill grade returning. The thunder of hoofs and the cries of the hat-waving spectators loosed a hidden reserve of speed and he flashed across the finish line the winner by a slim margin.

"I beat him by a coopla' steps," Bill said, in his rich Irish accent.

"What did you win?"

"Some gold pieces and lots of drinks," Bill replied, grinning.

Few towns were densely populated enough to support one, so Harold Clark was eastern Oregon's traveling dentist. In 1901, he had a classy, fast-stepping team and buggy he used in making his rounds. As one lady told me, "Many of the old-timers still carry his work around in their mouths."

An interesting contributor in her sixties, Freda McDaniels, told of the time Doc Coe, Bend's pioneer doctor, was out on his rounds beyond the town of Laidlaw, towards Gist. "My dad, Mr. Clark, was getting one of his fields fenced off where the road had been cutting one corner," she said. "To get the travelers used to the idea, he laid several logs across the lane. He was busy stringing barbed wire, and didn't see Doc returning, asleep at the reins. The horse slowed a little, looked the roadblock over, and plowed right through. The good doctor was almost pitched out on his head as the wagon lurched over the log."

Freda's brother, Cleon Clark, was the first white baby to be born in Laidlaw. The townspeople told his folks that if they named him after the town, they would donate a lot to the new boy. The folks thought it over, but just gave him the initial "L," so he didn't get the plot. The boy later took the middle name of Ladd, though.

Of course, there was hot rivalry among the new towns to entice newcomers, and each hamlet, for a few years, had its own newspaper. One of the more popular and likable editors in those robust days was Mr. LaFollette, of La Pine. They still talk about the time he put the sign in his window, or on the door, notifying everyone he had taken leave of the inkpots, with the following:

**You all liked last week's edition of the paper so well,
I had it printed up as it was and sent out again.**

LaFollette Gone Fishing

The men of the town had their innings sometime later when they gathered oatmeal boxes in small and large size, painted them red, then dummied them up with rope fuses. The pranksters got in a group, marched up to the front of the newspaper office, loudly crying, "We're gonna blow up this damn paper, and the editor too!" As they lit matches to set off the fake bombs, feet were flying out the back, through the screen door and all.

At a meeting of the city fathers in early-day Bend, among things discussed was the opening of another den of iniquity housing scarlet women. The building was well hidden by a fringe of junipers at what is now Third and Franklin. Discussion was not going too well and heads were merely nodded as one persistent member kept bringing the subject up. As the meeting was closing, he left with the parting shot, "I'm going to investigate!"

With more naivety than good sense, he did.

Quite late that next night, a small figure was feeling his way through the junipers as quietly as a night moth. An elfin glimmer of a light was his destination. When he got within the shadow of the building, he stumbled over some obstacle and, from several upstairs windows, got the contents of thunder mugs tossed all over him.

The girls had been tipped off.

The man fled in a panic, falling, rolling amid shrieks of girlish laughter behind him. It was late, but with visions of every foul disease known to the mind of man crawling over him, he had to get disinfected, so off he streaked to look up a doctor.

The young locals made their spending money in various ways. Ivan McGillvray and Hal Hoss cleaned lamp chimneys, split a pile of kindling by each stove in the rooms, lit gas lights in the lobby and dining rooms, and filled water pitchers on each room stand at the second of the early Pilot Butte Inns.

Paul Brooking of Bend and a buddy were janitors for many months at the old Central School — this while attending. Many of these people later ran businesses in central Oregon towns. Mr. Hoss later became one of

Oregon's first Secretaries of State.

At one time, the O'Kane Hotel of Bend had a man registered as "Philip Augustus, Emperor of the West." He was a fast talker and always trying to hire hands for work projects he had, but few took the jobs because the pay was poor.

Hugh O'Kane, the hotel owner, in later years was a rotund man with several chins. On warm afternoons, he would doze on a tipped-back chair in front of his establishment. One particular paper boy used to delight in folding the paper (*The Bulletin*) and carefully inserting it in under his chin where the man would find it upon awakening.

When the stages and the trains came in, each hotel had a man hired to greet newcomers as they hopped off into the new town of Bend. Each man had his own particular spiel and style to lure customers to his hostelry. Maurice Cashman was one of these verbal admen who parlayed his personality and business acumen into running what was for years central Oregon's largest men's store, Cashman's Clothiers.

After the pilgrims got their supplies and headed for their outpost, it might be weeks or months before they got another look at the thin veneer of civilization. But it wasn't always just supplies that brought them back to town again.

The long arm of the law reached out into the sagelands when need be. Thus it was that a Wagontire rancher, Tom, stopped one day to help a fellow rancher, Charlie, sitting in the middle of the Bend-Burns highway, holding his head.

Charlie had lost his hat, and that hat had character — 14 years of it. But it seems that he was in the hat when he lost it. His Model T had jackknifed on a rock and they both flew out and sat there as puddles of gas from the tank under the seat and the brass radiator's water drained out into the desert sands. Charlie held a handkerchief to a bad gash in his head. As he bound up his wrist and head, Tom asked Charlie what his hurry had been.

"I bin supeenied!" Charlie moaned. "I got t'git t' Bend by 10 o'clock to testify."

"I'll get you there," Tom volunteered. "Just help me tip your lizzie up again on its wheels and I'll tow you there. I'll keep a tight chain on 'er!''

That last was the understatement of the year.

They were off in a cloud of central Oregon dust — no different than any other dust, except there was more of it. All the ailing Charlie could do was get what air he could, turn the wheel from side to side, estimate the play in the steering wheel, and ride the brakes. He couldn't see anything but the rear end of the truck intermittently through eyes that watered from gasoline fumes and swirling dust. His split head throbbed and his stomach was cold in its pit from that wild ride.

After an hour's ride, they were slowing down, so Charlie rode the flimsy brakes harder. The two cars came to rest with a resounding crash in front of P. B. Johnson's store at Millican. When the air cleared, Charlie crawled underneath the Ford, muttering to himself that he had had enough of this madness, and tried to unfasten the chain. His miserable condition hampered his best efforts in this direction, when he heard Tom yell ''here we go!'' and saw him go by in three bounds. He had merely stopped for a new plug of tobacco.

Charlie scrambled out from under his Ford in a panic and a fury as it lurched forward with a sickening jerk. Three or four remarkable leaps of his own caught the top that was folded back so he could clamber in and take the wheel again. They were heading for the nightmare ride down Horse Ridge, a bad ride under the best of conditions, before leveling off on the juniper flat approaching the sentinel, Pilot Butte.

Many terrific jolts later, with Charlie riding the brakes with a vengeance and Tom stamping the foot feed, they hove into Bend. Convinced by now that this helping hand had a bad case of warts, Charlie didn't even bother to look back at his benefactor as they pulled up in front of the old courthouse. He bounded up the steps so justice could be done, hardly looking the part of a court witness, nor possessing one vestige of dignity. He looked as if he had been shot out of a cannon.

Whatever happened at the trial was an anticlimax. Charlie's hair was coiffed in sand and blood, his face gray with pumice dust that gave him the look of a voodoo priest.

The bandage was dried brown with blood atop his head, and the handkerchief on his wrist was unmentionable. As he moved from room to room looking for the judge's chambers, skirts swirled, buns came undone, pencils dropped, and doors slammed. Those with an affinity for shuffling papers were ruffling the edges. Snickers were skittering from room to room with him, which isn't at all proper for anything pertaining to a court of law. But no doubt, in the end, justice was done — it usually is.

As mentioned earlier, many didn't see the lights of town for months at a time. Along about March, supplies were usually running out in one direction or another. It might be lard, sugar, or saleratus. Whatever it was, it put a crimp in the fare the cook dished out.

When things got bad enough, the wife finally made mention of her plight to the old man.

But the snow melt is on and there are a million things to do with spring approaching, the husband says, so the plea is ignored. A few days later, another try, with the same results.

By now, another item in short supply is on the list. Now the old lady has *her* hackles up, so she clams up but is ready to consign the reprobate husband to the netherworld. Then one of the kids comes in to get a handful of cookies, and casually mentions, "Pa broke his pipe, and he's sure cussin' — "

"Put some of those cookies back!" the mother shouts. "Just a minute — what did you say?"

"Pa dropped his pipe in the mud and stepped on it and broke it."

Now this is too good. Someone will squirm before this is over. A luscious supper with some rare extras is fixed for the condemned. But the little lady is careful to notice —no after-dinner pipe.

A man without tobacco is a terror, but she can't resist a barb.

"You done smoking already?"

"I didn't smoke; my damn pipe's broke."

"Oh! That's a shame!"

Now it's the husband's turn to beg to go to town, but the wife says she'll substitute until

blue in the face. And the knack of a woman with a mean mind, she lays a flock of dress patterns out on the sitting room floor for an excuse of a day or two more delay.

"Let's go to town tomorrow," he pleads.

"I can't now. I'm making Sue some dresses."

"They can wait, can't they?"

(They could, but he didn't have to know it.)

Finally they are loaded up; the list has a pipe (or three or four) on it. The kids might get some Green River pop and see a Ken Maynard cowboy show. Ma brings eggs to sell and some of her fancy work for trade at Lara's store.

Have I forgotten anything?

In the central Oregon villages at the turn of the century, the deceased were sometimes handled by primitive methods. One bitterly cold night, Hugh Dugan, of Bend, was called by a local burial firm to pick up a stiff. (In that weather, it was literally — and figuratively — a stiff.) Unusually, the country had been bathed in rain for days, and Bend's streets, never good, were atrocious, with the rocks washed clean and upright and jagged and the mudholes deepened beyond belief. Then the freeze came.

This was the night that Hugh took off in the mortician's new Model T truck.

Now, he was familiar with the new shift-lever cars, but had never driven a Model T with its intricacies of footwork to send it in the right direction. "Low, reverse, and high" might just as well have been "high, wide, and handsome" to Hugh. He got to the unfortunate corpse and picked it up without too much trouble, but on the way back, with the body bouncing all over the wooden bed, Hugh must have come apart a little at the seams. The condition of the streets was unbelievable and being a Christian man, he was concerned with the welfare of the deceased.

"I got started and looked back and thought I'd break a hand or arm off, but I couldn't slow that damn truck down," Hugh said. "I went around that block three times because I couldn't find reverse or the brakes, and all the while the corpse was a good foot in the air

Top: North side of the second Pilot Butte Inn, Bend, 1908. Looking south on Wall Street. It was later called the Colonial Inn. Railroad men stayed here when in Bend.

most of the time.''

In another instance, Grandpa Green, a resident of the Hampton Butte area, died; the news spread rapidly because he was known and loved by all his neighbors. But with the funeral about due, it was discovered that there was no coffin. Lumber, as usual, was mighty scarce way out there. The problem might never have been solved except for a young rancher by the name of Langford. He

had just completed a horses' drinking trough, made of center-matched plank. He volunteered to give it up for the service.

They had already sent for Mr. Fogg, the preacher, from the east side of the butte, to add a religious touch; he was a man that had a way with words. As he talked, a small dust devil swirled by, maybe taking grandpa's spirit away. The men shifted from one foot to the other. Another small play of wind swirled as they filed by, and the old man was buried, the dirt thumping softly off the new planks of the horse trough, now put to a nobler use.

The earth murmured with their departing feet. It was a desert burial. And there were to be, in all the waiting earth, graves for them, too.

The local stores got most of the business, but the valley stores prevailed on the hop-picking trips there.

Dean Hollinshead said, "We generally had two wagons. We always stopped at Soap Creek on the way over, where us kids all had to take baths. Dad gave our grocery list to two different stores, and the one with the best price got the order."

Van Lake of the Hampton Butte sector did some reminiscing, too with a twinkle in his eye: "When we had teams, we went to town twice a year. Finally, when we had a Model T touring car, we found 'business' to attend to every two weeks. We went riding around town like big shots."

A winter trip to town, by sleigh, was remembered by Dean, a tall, spare ex-team-ster. "It was cold, and I was covered with quilts in the back," he said. "We'd go so far, and dad would take a nip. After he set the bottle down behind him, I'd take one too. After a few miles, the cold congealed him, so another shot was in order. I'd take a belt too. Many nips and many miles later, we got home. Dad could really hold his liquor, but I staggered out of that sleigh as crocked as they make 'em."

Dale Tussing had his homestead out near the two pines southwest of Brothers. (Actually, they weren't both pines; one was a large juniper.) Dale bought four quarts of good Canadian whiskey before he joined the army in World War I. He buried them on his place under a large, flat lava rock. He went to war and, on his return, opened up the shack again, visited his neighbors, and made a date with a friend or two. He dug up one bottle, and his buddies added to the beverages. Not long afterward, he got work in Bend, sold his place, and, while Dale was gone, the new owner started to level land and move rocks. It was a day of calamity. You guessed it. Three

A rowboat in the snow was the La Pine taxi service. (Slick Raper photo)

quarts of good Canadian whiskey are still buried somewhere out near two pines on the hill overlooking the vast face of the desert. The rock marker is moved to a new place, but the unrecovered liquor will age well.

Also during those World War I days, oleo was substituted for butter, about two pounds to one. At one sheep camp, the fellows got their heads together, ate the preferred butter first, and used the wrappers to put on the colorless substitute for a fake setup. When the rancher thumped in to eat, the hands were all gone. In the course of the meal, he noticed the anemic-looking butter. The next trip to town, he bumped into the creamery man on the main street and, in front of many townspeople, proceeded to bawl the hell out of him for forgetting to put coloring in his butter. The bewildered fellow stalked off, scratching his head, still not sure what had happened.

Basket socials, wherever they were held, were mighty popular. Orissa Sears said it wasn't so much looking over the crop of girls as getting the first square meal in weeks that got the bachelors to attend these so regularly. Maybe she was right, because most of them showed the whites of their eyes when a woman got near them, like a desert horse with a rope on it the first time.

These affairs were the safety valves to keep settlers from fractured nerves, especially the women. The girls of the sagebrush sorority brought the goodies. No questions were asked about the potables and viands if they were out of bounds or out of season. That just added to the merriment, like stolen apples.

Their feet were quickened with music and their mouths filled with laughter. Music was locally rendered. The Cal Sherman family have a Bressia violin, circa 1590, that was used often at these functions. Jim Benham, of Benham Falls, Benham Butte, used to make handmade violins of juniper wood. He came by his wood-carving skills naturally — he lost his leg in a hunting accident and whittled the substitute himself.

A woman from La Pine remembered, "We danced all night, many times on wooden sidewalks, and had venison steaks for breakfast." Karl Kleinfeldt added to that by saying, "The reason we danced all night was that we had no headlights on the horses."

Baby sitters came a few generations later; at these affairs, the kids all came. But even they finally ran down, crawled under blankets in wagons in the summer or slept on benches on the inside in cold weather.

The feeds were something to behold. Ham, sausage, bacon, venison, and eggs started things off. Spuds were raw-fried and American-fried in ham fat or bacon grease. If someone remembered to bring the sourdough for biscuits, that was the special for the morning. Otherwise it was quick bread, saleratus-type, or great mouth-watering slabs of fluffy homemade loaves.

Each young housewife had her speciality in jams or jellies, and these were liberally displayed along the tables. If someone had recently found a bee tree, a hollow juniper near an irrigation ditch, the honey ranked high on the list of sweets. There used to be dozens of these trees in eastern Oregon before the disease of foul brood got into all the hollow trees and killed most of the bee population.

Where there was a lack of greens, pickles filled the bill. Pickles of every kind: dill, sweet, bread and butter, watermelon, beet, crab apple, and mustard. Pickled carrots, pears, peaches, and figs were also there, including piccalilli, relish, chowchow, and chutney.

Pies, cakes, cookies, and doughnuts sent people reeling from the tables. It was no wonder the vittles enticed the gun-shy bachelors when all other wiles failed.

When the last of the tempting smells of homeground coffee and steak spattering in the fry pans had awakened the sleepiest kids to wind them up again, the folks knotted together in groups planning upcoming work projects, talking barter since cold cash was cherished for special emergencies.

Everyone was a neighbor. Karl Kleinfeldt said it very simply: "If you weren't a neighbor, you didn't have any neighbors."

The women swapped recipes and young brides were desperately trying to learn the seemingly vague mysteries of sourdough biscuits. There was a rumor, batted about from Wagontire to Shaniko, that some of these biscuits were so light they couldn't be made on a windy day or they would be blown off the plates.

This yarn about biscuits is probably in the same category as the one about the cow, a fine milker, that died suddenly. Until a new one could be found, the owners took the hide and stretched it on a fence in a shady place and milked it for three days until the new replacement arrived.

Another tale was told about one family in the sagelands that appropriated any stray calf that wandered by. It was kept in the dugout or root cellar. Juniper limbs were dragged over its tracks so the trail bypassed their place. When the heat was off, the calf was butchered.

No matter.

Most cattlemen laugh about not knowing how *their* beef tastes — they never do, because they always eat their neighbor's.

Mrs. Stella Nelson told about one of her neighbors, Gus Grill, an Austrian, who was the strongest man she ever saw. He lived a mile and a half from the road the wagons used. When his flour was delivered, he bent over at the waist while they loaded the flour sacks onto him. Four, sometimes five, one-hundred-pound sacks were put on him, one on each shoulder, one across behind his neck, and the other two straddling those three. "We saw this many times," Mrs. Nelson said. "He carried them that way to his shack." This man lived in the Brothers area.

Mrs. Nelson also recalled the time Bill Brown, "the horse king," came by their house the first time. "He had one shoe on and the other one off," she said. "That time, he was riding horseback — he generally walked. He had heard about my carrot pie and had come over for some, because he dearly loved carrot pie. From then on, I always had to leave carrot pie on the table for Bill, and he left money. Whenever he was near Brothers, he came by and had two or three pieces of it."

There was the time that four bankers rode out into the desert to buy Bill out. He got wind of it, filled his pack, probably with raisins, because they were regular fare for him, and walked off into the nowhere of the desert. There he stayed for a week or more until they gave up looking for him.

The offer? $350,000.

Ray Markham of Bend freighted for "the horse king" when he was in the sheep business. "This stuff about his writing checks on tomato can wrappers, paper sacks, or tops of shoe boxes is true. I saw him do it dozens of times. If someone took a notion to quit or draw some pay, it might be miles from anywhere, so whatever paper was handy was used." These slips were all honored by the banks.

Bill made his fortune in wild horses, selling to the Allies during World War I. France got many of them.

Bill would buy a horse that took his fancy right on the spot. More than one stranger took advantage of this by riding into camp in the dim light of a campfire with a fine-looking mount. If Bill took a shine to it, he would buy it "right now." But the stranger would be careful to keep the branded side in the dark, and Bill would grin sheepishly at himself in the morning to see his own brand on the broomtail, the famous horseshoe brand.

Another story relates how one night after a supper of beans, biscuits, and antelope steaks, Bill's riders were sitting around the

Lizard Creek, near Hampton Butte, 4th of July celebration in 1912. Truck is the Bend-Burns Stage. (Brookings photo)

Jim Benham and Marsh Awbrey (in buggy), both noted Central Oregon pioneers and ranchers. 1910. (Al Moore photo)

fire rolling their own and filling their pipes with P. A. or Tuxedo.

"Bill, since you're the horse king of the west and have handled thousands of them, what do you do for a horse that slobbers?" one of the men asked.

"I reckon I don't know," Bill said.

"Teach him t' spit!"

Another early settler who almost became a legend in his own time was Marsh Awbrey. A small, wiry man who was Indian fighter, government scout, cattleman and horseman extraordinary, he rode more miles horseback and camped out oftener than almost any rancher in the period 1880-1920. Awbrey wore a little black felt hat and had most of his clothes made by hand, probably because he was so small. He had to mount from a stump or windfall when he could. He was fond of Indian-style clothes, and, like Walt McCoin and several other early-day cowboys, wore the traditional red kerchief around his neck.

Awbrey's horses were superb animals, and he took the best care of them. On his famous ride from his White Rock Ranch north of Laidlaw (now Tumalo) to Eugene, Awbrey used a long-limbed favorite named Giraffe. This ride, made from sunup to sunset, was to see his mother after he got word she was quite sick. He went the general route of the present-day McKenzie highway, but knew many shortcuts. The McKenzie runs through the roughest, most terrible lava flow in the Cascades. It was a terror on horses. Awbrey seldom galloped a horse. On that legendary ride to the valley, he trotted his horse.

A habit of Awbrey's, still remembered by some Bend residents, was the way he kissed a five- or ten-dollar gold piece good-bye before handing it to a clerk. He never failed in this.

Alfred Moore, an early-day postman, told the touching tale of the day Mr. Awbrey left Bend. He was elderly and, some thought, unable to take good care of himself, so arrangements were made to put him in a veteran's hospital in the valley. Awbrey knew he was leaving his beloved ranch, and his horses, and the land he had ridden for uncounted miles, in good times and bad. From the timber's edge to the sun-washed deck of the Great Basin had been his domain. All this must have been passing through his mind, of the times he had looked with a cold, proud eye on this land immured in silence.

It took four men to put him on the train. He weighed but 125 pounds. It was a sad ending for a robust, hell-for-leather pioneer who did much toward colonizing this land with fine cattle and horses.

Fine cowboys rode in the days of the wild horse roundups. For unnumbered months, their wild "yippees" sang across the stillness of the desert scabland, amid the dull thunder of hoofs and rolling clouds of dust. And there were the never-ending stories.

It was not all business and rough and hard work. The pilgrims, and young fellows especially, were good marks for many tales merely edged with the truth.

There was a rider who had a short forefinger that was a natural for them to spin yarns about.

"See that guy settin' by the fire?" someone would ask. "I'll tell you how he got that short forefinger. He used to be a guide in the Grand Canyon pointin' out scenery to visitin' folks. When he wore it off to the first knuckle, they retired him on disability, 'fore it got any shorter."

In talking to many of the older generation, there were bound to be some colorful expressions. Some slipped out and others were remembered and told of their neighbors. "The spuds didn't manure very well this year; the season was too short," one person said. Or "He got a new car, and it's got suspender springs and bloomer tires." Again: "He was coming down the road with his lizzie and came to a mudhole, but he put 'er in mutual, and she went right through." Another man, telling of his hunting rifle, said it was a 45/90, and making a circle with his thumb and forefinger, showed it had an oxygen barrel so big . . . . One sharp character said he bought sharp-nosed cattle to eat

safely between the sharp rocks on his place. And finally: "In the thirties, one family got one of them new electric ice boxes, but then, when we moved it in, we tipped it and all the pneumonia ran out of it."

These folks may have missed a word now and then, but all were genuine people, and many had shrewd business heads.

Typical is the case of a fellow who had a beautiful mare pastured in a field bordering the road around Pilot Butte where many passerby saw her. In less than a week, someone stopped by, looked around a bit, and finally went to town to learn who owned the horse.

The two men came back with a veterinarian and, between them, they looked her over from fetlock to teeth, and the deal was made.

But a few days later, one mad purchaser, with the sheriff in tow, came looking up the former owner with the idea of making an arrest.

"Did you sell this man this horse?" the sheriff asked.

"Yes, I did."

"He wants his money back."

"He ain't gonna git it."

"Well, he can't use the horse the way she is."

"That's not my fault; they looked her all over."

"He had a vet with him so he wouldn't get stuck," the seller said. "They trotted her around, looked at her teeth, and listened to her wind."

With that, the sheriff turned and stomped off.

It turned out the mare was blind, and neither one could spot that.

Shrewd businessmen, they were.

But the thin years were over. The depression was ended when one morning a settler looked out of his kitchen window and saw a jackrabbit loping across the desert without two homesteaders chasing it.

When the going got too rough for those turning close to their sixties or seventies, they reluctantly moved to town. They soon had a favorite hangout where they discovered other oldsters congregated. Here they loved to talk of the good old days. One old man, in his eighties and getting just a wee bit forgetful, made his morning trip downtown one beautiful June morning to Bill Baer's Waldorf.

He asked the bartender, "What day is this, Bill?"

"The 15th of November," the bartender kidded him.

"The hell it is! Where has the summer gone!"

It was here the oldsters discovered subtle changes. Their once-familiar breakfast, dinner, and supper were now dubbed luncheon and dinner. But with a quite rebellion, most retained the older flavors as long as they lived.

The long-houred ranching days kept the settlers as spare as their juniper fence posts, to match the growth beyond the ponderosa country — sparse. The soft gray-green desert blanket suited the eye but did little to fatten a pocketbook.

So the once magnificent dream ended and the bubble burst.

The gardens withered, and the stark fact of an empty pantry and bare bank account forced them inevitably to town, to the mills.

Nothing much has changed now. The once-naked shingles are richened with a cover of lichens and moss to bright green and drab orange. If we could walk back into those yesterdays, down, down the dusty road, we could see these unpainted shacks, gleaming in a high sun. We could see sleighs disappearing in a swirl of snow and other snows melted, settled, caked, and covered again with tawny sands drifting across them. We could see a sheepman twisting off a dead juniper limb, cursing its incredible toughness, frustrating his quick fire. We could see the white flanks of antelope, floating across the horizon, and see the wild horses — drinkers of the wind — loping ahead of their dusts to a hidden waterhole. And see a burnt-cheeked boy lying on his back under an aged patriarch, chewing on the sweetness of a cheatgrass stalk.

The staples, driven by a hundred gnarled hands, now loosen in weathered juniper posts. The rabbit brush obscures the high plans for streets once graded. As the towns grew, dozens of obscure lives perished in anonymity. Others were moved to — who cares where? Where the old residences fall, there moves progress.

To the west, overnight, those renegades, Three Fingered Jack and Bachelor, flirt with the Sisters dressed in the serene whiteness of their winter finery. The mule deer drift downward; the small creatures etch their nameplates across this wilderness, to all who can read. Slowly, imperceptably, the sulking sun climbs in the south to bring the honeyed taste of spring. April breathes upon the hills to rouse the junipers from their sleep. But in a typical central Oregon spring, the air is thinned with cold; six more weeks, a wind knifes across the land, now slowly stirring. On the brow of a hill, the day is born, but the settlers are no more. They have gone.

APPENDIX A

Barbed Wire Boothills

From the people talked to, in the course of writing this book, there was a constant flow of information about pioneer grave sites, most of them little known, unkempt, grown over with bunchgrass, and unmarked with headstones. Some were formerly fenced and given a semblance of protection by nearby settlers, but as the small ranch gave way to the bank and finance company cattle corporations, personalities, dead or alive, count for less.

The fenced grave plots are convenient rubbing posts for wandering cattle and the fences are eventually pushed over. What headstones were once standing are now trodden in the sands.

For what it is worth, a small appendix of known burial grounds is here listed.

There are many buried in ranch yards from epidemics in the Silver Lake area.

There are some marked graves on the Gowdy Ranch.

At the former Price place, there are the graves of two Indians and one 14-year-old white girl, crushed by her falling horse on the way to school.

There are eight graves on the Cunningham Ranch, N.W. corner of N.W. Section 24, Township 20, Range 20.

An old cemetery can be found near the mouth of Camp Creek on the Barnes place.

Near Buck Creek of the Silver Lake area, two miles from bench, there are some plots.

A board marker can be seen near Walker Well.

An Indian grave can be found at Skull Hollow, Gray Butte; and another at Cultus Mountain.

There are eight known Allen graves at Little River above old Camp Abbot.

The old Shepherd place, at Powell Butte, has one grave.

On the original Sherman place, in the high desert, there are two graves.

Camp Polk has some military graves.

There are 12 graves of the Zumwalt family in the Sisters area.

On the Springer place, near the Gist post office, can be found five graves.

Bunchgrass waves over yet-undiscovered graves, even as the wind thrums through nearby telephone wires. So few of them were brushed by immortality that they now lie forgotten in their own private barbed wire boothills.

APPENDIX B

Pioneer Teachers

Mrs. Aldrich
Mrs. Alfrey
Mrs. Ashbaugh — Halfway House
Tillie Balfor
Anna Beaver
Miss Bell — Fort Rock
Ida Blevins — Culver
Mr. Boegli — Prineville
Paul Bratton — Silver Lake area
Carrie Bridges — Plainview
Alice Brookings — Halfway House
Marie Brosterhous — Cline Falls
Warren Brown — Old Collver
Emma Buchanan — Sisters
Oscar Butzien — Halfway House
Mrs. Cady
Mrs. Grover Caldwell — Shevlin Camps,
    Ryan Ranch
Mr. Clark
Marion Coe — Bend-Redmond
Grace Cook — Laidlaw
Jenny Creighton — Silver Lake
Effie Crooks — Prineville
Mrs. Derrick — Fremont
Mrs. Dillon — Crooked River, 11 miles
    downriver, Prineville
Charles Dinwitty — Gray Butte
Harriet Dolson — Silver Lake
Helen Douthit — Culver
Mrs. Judy Duffy
F. A. Everett — Horse Ranch, Fort Rock
Mrs. Farney — Lower Bridge
Carrie Fee — Lava
Mr. Ford — Prineville
Roan Gideon — Powell Butte
Bertha Graham — Brothers
May Halbert
Mr. Hampton — log school (Bend?)
Miss Holmes — Fort Rock

Will Hoyt — Crooked River
Theodore Hubbard — Dry Lake
Florence Hunnel — Laidlaw
C. C. Jackson — Silver Lake
R. B. Jackson — Buck Creek
Mr. S. K. King
Miss Langford — Dry Lake
Charles Lewis — Culver
Mary Linster — Powell Butte
Mr. Lockrey
Esther McCaulley — Silver Lake
Mrs. McGillvray
Miss Martin — Old Collver
Mayfield — Powell Butte
Ed Merril — Culver
Herman Miller — Brothers
Mrs. Miller
Nettie Mitschler — Fort Rock
Mrs. Moehring
Letha Everett Morris
Mrs. Mortimer — Cabin Lake area
J. E. Myers — Powell Butte
L. A. Myers — Silver Lake
Ethel Odell — on the desert
E. E. Orton — Prineville
George Pauls — Haystack
Joe Perry — Culver
Flay Potter — Horse Ranch
Mary Priestoff
Minnie Raddatz — Brothers
Bertha Ransom
Mr. Redman — La Pine
Mrs. Reed
Nona Richardson — Silver Lake-Fremont
    area
George Ridgway — Gray Butte
Mr. and Mrs. Glen Slack — Bend and other
    places
Viola Smith — Imperial

Mary Stauffer — Brothers-Stauffer area
Mrs. Steve Steidl — Cline Falls
A. C. Strange — Prineville
John Tuck — Montgomery School
Lily Turner
Jenny Walton

Montell Weist — Bend-Redmond
Mrs. West — Silver Lake
Rex Whittaker — Dry Lake
Mr. Wilcox — Powell Butte
Tiller Wilson — Sisters

APPENDIX C

Central Oregon Ghost Towns or Towns Once Having a Post Office

Arrow — post office, Lake County

Barnes — post office, north between Millican and Brothers

Camp Polk — post office, military, north of Sisters

Cline Falls —post office, west of Redmond on the Deschutes

Connley —post office

Crook —post office, near Prineville

Cross Keys — post office, near Cow Canyon, north of Madras

Desert — post office, between Prineville and Warm Springs

Echo —post office, desert town east of Bend

Farewell Bend — post office, predecessor to Bend

Fife — post office, between Millican and Brothers, north

Fleetwood — post office, east of Fort Rock

Forest — post office, near Lone Pine

Garrison — post office

Gist — post office, between Laidlaw (Tumalo) and Sisters

Greendale — post office, Fort Rock area

Harper — post office, near Abbot

Harris Place — post office

Haystack — post office, southeast of Culver, perhaps the oldest

Held — post office, north of Dry Lake near Brothers, named after Paul Held

Howard — post office, east of Prineville

Imperial

Kirk — post office, near Haystack

Laidlaw — post office, now Tumalo, named after W.A. Laidlaw

Lake — post office

LaMonta — post office

Luna Vista — post office, Fort Rock sector

Lytle — post office, early Bend addition

Mecca — post office, north of Warm Springs, on the Deschutes (a crossing)

Mowry — post office, Beaver Creek

O'Dell — post office

O'Neil

Opal City — post office, north of Culver, was a railroad section stop

Palmain — post office, was Willow Creek Basin, now Madras

Pelton — post office, near Willow Creek

Polk — post office

Pringle Flat — post office

Roberts — post office, near Camp Creek

Rolyat — Halfway House (Rolyat is Taylor spelled backwards)

Staats — may have been a post office, addition to Bend

Stauffer — post office, south of Brothers

Wakefield — post office

Wastina — post office, Fork Rock, Silver Lake country

Weimer — post office near Laidlaw

Weisteria — addition to early Bend

Bibliography

Cheney, W. D. *The Bend Book*. Bend Park Company, 1911.

An Illustrated History of Central Oregon. Spokane, Wash.: Western Historical Publishing Co., 1905.

"Many Hands." *Jefferson County Reminiscenses*. Portland, Or.: Binfords & Mort, 1957.

Seaman, N. G. *Indian Relics of the Pacific Northwest*. Portland, Or.: Binfords & Mort, 1946.

Ward, R. A. *The Western Tourist*, October 20, 1920, vol. I, no. 1.

Index